1996

University of St. Francis
G-CE
Good
Prog

P9-AOM-282

3 0301 00072761 6

PROGRAM DEVELOPMENT
IN
CONTINUING EDUCATION

The Professional Practices in Adult Education and Human Resource Development Series explores issues and concerns of practitioners who work in the broad range of settings in adult and continuing education and human resource development.

The books are intended to provide information and strategies on how to make practice more effective for professionals and those they serve. They are written from a practical viewpoint and provide a forum for instructors, administrators, policy makers, counselors, trainers, managers, program and organizational developers, instructional designers, and other related professionals.

Editorial correspondence should be sent to the Editor-in-Chief:

Michael W. Galbraith
Florida Atlantic University
Department of Educational Leadership
College of Education
Boca Raton, FL 33431

PROGRAM DEVELOPMENT IN CONTINUING EDUCATION

Allan E. Goody
Charles E. Kozoll

University of Illinois at Urbana-Champaign

LIBRARY
College of St. Francis
JOLIET, ILLINOIS

KRIEGER PUBLISHING COMPANY
MALABAR, FLORIDA
1995

Original Edition 1995

Printed and Published by
KRIEGER PUBLISHING COMPANY
KRIEGER DRIVE
MALABAR, FLORIDA 32950

Copyright © 1995 by Allan E. Goody and Charles E. Kozoll

All rights reserved. No part of this book may be reproduced in any form or
by any means, electronic or mechanical, including information storage and
retrieval systems without permission in writing from the publisher.
*No liability is assumed with respect to the use of the information contained
herein.*
Printed in the United States of America

FROM A DECLARATION OF PRINCIPLES JOINTLY ADOPTED BY A
COMMITTEE OF THE AMERICAN BAR ASSOCIATION AND COMMIT-
TEE OF PUBLISHERS:

This Publication is designed to provide accurate and authoritative information in re-
gard to the subject matter covered. It is sold with the understanding that the publisher is not engaged in rendering legal, accounting, or other professional service. If
legal advice or other expert assistance is required, the services of a competent professional person should be sought.

Library of Congress Cataloging-in-Publication Data

Goody, Allan E.
    Program development in continuing education / Allan E. Goody,
Charles E. Kozoll. —Original ed.
        p. cm.—(The Professional practices in adult education and human re-
source development series)
    Includes bibliographical references (p.) and index.
    ISBN 0-89464-852-7 (alk. paper)
    1. Continuing education—United States—Planning.   2. Continuing
education—United States—Administration.   I. Kozoll, Charles E.
II. Title. III. Series.
LC5251.G646 1995
374′.973—dc20   94-47469
                                                                          CIP

10 9 8 7 6 5 4 3 2

G-CE
374
G658

$19.50

Gueulan

4-17-96

156, 437

CONTENTS

PREFACE

Continuing education has become the largest of all of the educational enterprises in this country, if not throughout the world. The continuing education program is a broad term that encompasses many educational experiences. The program may be a workshop, seminar, professional meeting, conference, short course, even an educational tour. It could be held in the facilities of the sponsor or in a hotel, conference center, school, or community center. A continuing education program may be a simple one-hour lecture or it may be a complex conference that requires setting up a temporary organization and coordinating the work of many people.

No matter what name is attached to the program, or how complex it is, each is an educational experience that involves critical planning decisions, some of which we come to accept as routine and expect to arise in the normal course of planning. Other decisions will arise quite unexpectedly, but nonetheless requiring considered attention to ensure program success.

Today, more than ever, cosponsors have to be secured, financial support obtained and managed, and effective marketing done. The planning process will involve conflict including, perhaps, major and minor disagreements over purpose and agendas, and arguments about what will be served at meals. Conflict has to be managed and resolved. Planning is not for the faint of heart. Be prepared for disputes, surprises, and challenges.

In this book, continuing education program development and planning will be described and analyzed. Our goal is to equip readers with information and strategies they can use to plan programs such as the one in the first example described below, and avoid the disappointment related to the second one.

- For nearly fifty years, about 100 senior maintenance supervisors at correctional institutions and hospitals spend a week at an educational conference in a retreat setting. Attendance has varied little during this lengthy period of time and some participants have been to more than half of the programs. Topics covered include latest changes in technology, techniques for motivating employees, and laws affecting their work. Because of the program's positive image, little marketing had to be done. In most years, the program made money.
- At the same time, a program for a similar group of maintenance supervisors at higher education institutions slowly collapsed. Over its nearly ten years of existence, the program had never had more than 30 people attending. Similar topics were covered, but the early emphasis was on so-called "soft skills" rather than technology-related topics. Each year, a very costly brochure had to be prepared and sent to thousands of potential participants. In spite of all the effort required, the return on investment was very low.

Why does the first program continue to thrive? Why did the second program experience so much difficulty before it was closed? A superficial review of both programs indicates that a planning process was in place for both programs. A closer examination would reveal certain gaps in the planning and overall position of the second program that led to its failure: the program concept was not clear; stronger competition was not recognized; and cosponsor support was very limited. Resources were directed at preserving the program rather than being innovative and responsive to change.

A large number of elements to be examined in this book have to be identified, organized and orchestrated to a successful conclusion, if programs are to be effective and well-received. Participants' motives for attending, program concept, and why different organizations choose to cosponsor a program must be clear. Even with all of this care and attention, the unpredictable is possible, in fact inevitable, and must be anticipated to the extent possible.

Of equal importance to all planning elements, we believe, are the roles leaders must play as programs are conceived, planned, and offered. Stress has been placed on where creative and management energy should be applied to make each program a success. The artistic dimension of program development cannot be forgotten. The phases of development to be described in the following chapters have an order and logic about them. There are, however, many relationships with cosponsors and others that have to be built and maintained. Those involved in planning must be kept informed and conflicts must be anticipated, where possible, and resolved. This will require a combination of human relations and political skills.

In the chapters to follow, we will address the content of programs, what planning steps are generic to continuing education, and how to deal with political dimensions that can be both a contribution and a potential disruptive force. You will find a description of our view of the development process in Chapter 1, how it can be viewed as five phases, and why we prefer the term "approaches" to "models." We also look at the role of the program planner and the knowledge and skills needed to plan successful programs. The importance of leadership is addressed.

Throughout this book we have referred to program development and program planning. Both terms broadly describe the entire process of creating and delivering a continuing education program. Using a narrower definition of the terms, the first two phases in the process we suggest in Chapter 1 could be considered program development, and the remaining three phases include activities associated with actually planning the program.

Building on the phases of program development and the role of the program planner in Chapter 1, we draw attention in Chapter 2 to some of the many challenges that are common when programs are planned. Confronting these challenges is just one part of your responsibilities in building a successful program.

The chapters that follow deal with the phases of program development that must be considered when programs are planned. They range from gathering information, to making a decision to move from program concept to planning, through budget management and marketing, to delivery of the program, and the mass of administrative details. The significance of each of the phases in development will vary from program to program.

Existing literature provides some guidance and support for

the necessary steps to be taken. When appropriate, that literature has been consulted and identified, but much of this book is derived from practice, both that of the authors and many colleagues.

We designed the book so that it would be of value to those with limited experience in developing and planning continuing education programs. We envisioned this book as a guide for those new to the field of continuing education program development, and for students enrolled in courses on program development. Unexpectedly, we found those with experience in planning who have read the book feel it is both a useful review for them and the source of many forgotten points and questions that should be considered in their planning work. We hope that all three groups will benefit from reading this material, weighing what is suggested, and using the ideas as the basis for their own planning and program management.

ACKNOWLEDGMENTS

We appreciate the contributions of a number of people who helped us a great deal as this book was conceived, written and shaped. Michael Galbraith provided us with clear guidance throughout the project. The Krieger staff were especially helpful as the book was being prepared for production. Graduate students in continuing education at the University of Illinois at Urbana-Champaign provided valuable feedback on the material covered in the book.

We are indebted to the reviews provided by our valued colleagues, Violet Malone of Western Washington University and Jim Pollicita of Miami University. Through their perceptive comments and useful suggestions, we were able to sharpen and further develop the manuscript. Many thanks as well to Shirley Fryer, Sheila Ryan, and Lynn Schaefer for their excellent editorial suggestions and to our families for their support and encouragement.

THE AUTHORS

Allan E. Goody served on the faculty of Curtin University of Technology in Perth, Western Australia, from 1982 to 1992. He resigned in 1992 to pursue full-time graduate studies in the United States. At Curtin he taught accounting, finance, taxation, and business law courses in the undergraduate agribusiness program at Muresk Institute of Agriculture and in university extension programs. He also developed and delivered courses for distance education students. Goody was awarded the inaugural Edwards Award in 1987 for teaching excellence.

Prior to his appointment at Curtin University, Goody practiced accountancy both in public practice and in corporations. He has a Bachelor of Business degree from the University of Southern Queensland (formerly Darling Downs Institute of Advanced Education), Toowoomba, Australia, and a Master's of Extension Education from the University of Illinois at Urbana-Champaign.

Currently, Goody is a doctoral student in the Department of Educational Organization and Leadership at the University of Illinois at Urbana-Champaign. He holds a graduate research assistantship in the department with responsibilities in program planning and administration. He was awarded a University Fellowship in 1993. Goody's research interests include program planning and the application of learning from professional development to improve practice, and faculty development.

Goody's experiences in continuing education and professional development include the development of short courses and seminars in adult and continuing education, training of trainers, and study tours. In 1989 he was a visiting scholar at the University of Illinois developing and administering courses for international extension agents. He has extensive experience in course development for undergraduate and graduate students and has taught program development courses at the University of Illinois.

Charles E. Kozoll is a professor of education and associate director of the Office of Continuing Education and Public Service (OCEPS) at the University of Illinois at Urbana-Champaign. In these positions, he has major administrative responsibility for a number of continuing education programs, in addition to teaching and advising masters and doctoral students. Kozoll's course areas are program planning and evaluation and human resource development. He has taught the course on program development in continuing education for the past 20 years.

In his role as associate director of OCEPS, he directs a statewide educational program for local government officials, serves as editor of two publication series, and assists in the development of noncredit programs for professional audiences. He also initiated ELDERHOSTEL programs at the university and a number of other programs for seniors. His most recent work involves research on how research studies can be provided to lay audiences in an understandable and useful form.

With a background in both adult learning and organizational psychology, Kozoll has worked closely with a number of private and public organizations to evaluate employee productivity, to present supervisory training programs, and to prepare a variety of training materials. His clients have included local, state, and federal government agencies, social service organizations, small product and service businesses, and educational institutions. He serves as a national lecturer on productivity for Phi Delta Kappa and is an associate in the Executive Development Center at the University of Illinois at Urbana-Champaign.

In addition to consulting, Kozoll has written on a variety of management related topics, with emphasis on training new employees, time and stress management, and developing supervisory skills. He has published eight books, over 200 articles, six software programs, and a videotape on time and stress management. His material has appeared in the publications of Dartnell Corporation, Bureau of Business Practice, the National Management Institute and The Alexander Hamilton Institute. He is a coauthor of *Professional Office Procedures* and *Top Performance,* a textbook and decision-making simulation, published by the Glencoe Division of Macmillan/McGraw-Hill book publishers in 1992. He currently is studying how effective in-organization training programs can be developed, and how and why both public and private organizations collaborate. Research in both areas will be published in 1996.

His degrees from the University of Michigan, Boston University, and Columbia University are in the areas of political science, adult learning, and organizational psychology.

CHAPTER 1

A Basic Approach: Five Phases of Program Development and the Role of the Program Planner

Developing effective continuing education programs requires both management skill and a combination of artistic and political ability. The management dimension is seen as programs are conceived, planned, and operated. Artistry appears as a total experience is created, one designed to leave a strong positive impression and memory among the program's participants. Political savvy is evident when conflicts are anticipated and resolved, relationships built, and groups with different agendas joined together, albeit temporarily, to plan a program that will bring luster to all those involved.

In this chapter, we will present an approach to developing and planning continuing education programs. It is an approach, not a prescriptive model of what should be done on all occasions. Continuing education programs share some similarities, in that they build on the participants' prior knowledge to some extent, are events usually distinct from the routine of those who attend them, and generally are short and focused events. Apart from these similarities, each one is unique.

We have divided the approach into five phases: generating ideas; identifying and obtaining the necessary resources; determining the potential for the program's success; completing the necessary planning, budgeting, marketing and administrative details; and conducting and evaluating the program and completing the postprogram wrap-up.

These phases, unfortunately, do not occur in a linear fashion. What may appear as a logical step-by-step process does not follow in practice. For example, you may be doing background research, constructing a budget, and searching for cosponsors at the same time. During development of the program, you will continually review the progress made and return to earlier decisions to make changes or to reaffirm the decision to go ahead. For example, you may return to the go/no-go decision quite often, and will be frequently identifying resources and making decisions about the directions the planning process is taking. Continuing education program planning is not neat and orderly. It is a very dynamic and very often unpredictable activity.

To complicate matters even more, each planner approaches planning with a different set of assumptions, personal philosophies, and experiences. Organizations sponsoring programs may have complicated procedures that must be followed. Each program, too, is unique: some will be very complicated, with many events, speakers, and unusual features, and others involve perhaps just one speaker and one room.

Planning programs has more of a "recipe" than a "prescription" dimension to it. Recipes can be modified to suit both the "cook's" and the recipients' tastes. Changes can be made to accommodate special situations. Prescriptions have a certain lockstep quality about them, mandating specific planning activities that may be sound but not always relevant.

The second part of the chapter addresses the roles of the program planner in the planning process. In addition to the six broad roles we identify, there are many activities relying on a variety of skills and knowledge. To conclude the chapter the important role that leadership plays in guiding the program development process is addressed.

FIVE PHASES OF PROGRAM DEVELOPMENT

Over the years that programs have been planned for adults, researchers studying the development and planning process have provided numerous approaches that we can consider and adapt to our task (Boone, 1985; Boyle 1981; Brookfield, 1986; Houle, 1972; Kidd, 1973; Knowles, 1980; Mezirow, 1963). These approaches mostly describe how planning should be done, rather than how it is done in practice (Sork & Caffarella, 1990).

In *The Design of Education,* Houle (1972) provides seven very important assumptions about the fundamental system of practice that must be recognized and understood, if programs are to be well planned:

1. Any episode of learning occurs in a specific situation and is profoundly influenced by that fact.

2. The analysis or planning of educational activities must be based on the realities of human experience and on constant change.

3. Education is a practical art.

4. Education is a cooperative rather than an operative art.

5. The planning or analysis of an educational activity is usually undertaken in terms of some period that the mind abstracts for analytical purposes from complicated reality.

6. The planning or analysis of an educational activity may be undertaken by an educator, a learner, an independent analyst, or some combination of the three.

7. Any design of education can best be understood as a complex of interacting elements, not as a sequence of events.

Careful reading of Houle's explanations of these seven assumptions reveals important elements, especially the dynamics of any planning process, and indeed the programs themselves. Programs are not insulated from the realities around them.

Using Houle's assumptions as a foundation, our approach to program development involves five phases. This approach best represents what is done in the planning process. It would be easy to represent what should be done in a flow diagram. But what is actually done in the development and planning process is far more complex, dynamic, and interactive, and is unique to each program. Many experienced planners we talked with commented on the reality represented in this five-phase approach.

Phase One: Generating Ideas

Many sources are possible for generating ideas. Evaluations from past programs is one. Planning committees that have traditionally been formed are a second source. An external grant may dictate, in part, what will be covered. The latest developments in research and technology or new legislation may create the need for a program. A newspaper article may generate an idea. Looking at the competition or comparable program offerings may identify possible program topics. These sources may lead to a well-developed concept for a program or just the germ of an idea. Idea generation could be done in one hour or take many months. The idea is the basis for sitting down and beginning the second phase.

Phase Two: Identifying and Obtaining Necessary Resources

Phase two involves a number of steps that include: reviewing who might participate in the program; how clearly participants can be identified and what their history of participation in comparable programs has been; identifying information and expertise available to address the topic; determining if an appropriate location(s) is available; examining the financial commitment needed and if there are funds currently or potentially available to make that commitment; and assessing the level of support for the program among primary and secondary sponsors. Consider what sacrifices of other programs will have to be made to accommodate this program. In this phase, an effort should be made to develop a clear concept for the program, describing how it will be unique and valuable.

In some cases, this phase is skipped entirely or substantially. For example, a professional association may have a well-established annual program, or a computer use course offered by a community college is always filled as soon as the announcement appears in the catalogue. A review and minimal work on the concept or focus of the program may be the only task.

This phase, however, will be very important when a new

program is planned or when a program with a shaky history is reviewed. Looking closely at potential viability is essential. A limited amount of background research can be done and discussions held. If the positives are stronger than the negatives, going ahead makes sense. Otherwise, this may be the point to stop.

Experienced program planners can relate how many times they have begun discussions with an individual who has an idea for a program. In a substantial number of cases, that first discussion identifies significant barriers to moving ahead: no clear group of participants; topic expertise not readily available; limited funds; no location that would be attractive to potential participants is available. Those involved in this discussion may discover just how much they disagree and how unwilling they are to continue the discussion. The person with the idea may go back to rethink the idea or just stop at this point.

Phrase Three: Determining the Potential for Success

Identifying resources and ensuring that they are available is not enough to guarantee program success. Phase three is focused heavily on determining the program's success potential. This step may not be necessary when a continuing education program has a history of success, or for example, when a program is fully funded by a sponsor for a distinct group of participants. When that history and support is absent, a substantial amount of background information will be needed. You also need to establish criteria for determining success. Look at success broadly, not just number of participants or financial results. Consider success in the long term as well as short term, such as relationships built and image developed. It is important to have appropriate evidence to support the success potential.

What to gather, what to do, and useful methods are more fully examined in Chapter 3. These steps include: market research to determine interest in the topic; environmental scanning to look at competition and similar offerings; and the use of advice from different sources.

At this time, a preliminary budget should be drafted. If a clear level of interest is determined and the budget seems realistic, making a commitment to the program is a sensible step. At this point in the planning, the go/no-go decision is critical. It is now that you will begin to spend real dollars and make firm commitments. Stopping at this point may be a very intelligent step to take.

Phase Four: Planning, Budgeting, Marketing, and Detail Management

In phase four, the active planning, program design, marketing, and completion of the many program details occur. Objectives are set, evaluations are developed, program content and learning activities are determined, and presenters chosen. A marketing plan is developed, a budget is set, and administrative arrangements are reviewed and carried out. Registration is conducted. At this time, a formative evaluation can be conducted to make sure that planning is proceeding effectively. These activities are described in detail in Chapters 4 through 6.

Phase Five: Conducting and Evaluating the Program and Wrap-up

The final phase is when the program is held and the many details associated with its operation are managed. Every effort is made to minimize problems, provide an excellent experience for all participants, and meet the program goals. A final evaluation is conducted and a financial report prepared. Letters of thanks are sent. A final report may be prepared. These activities are addressed in Chapter 7.

THE ROLES OF THE PROGRAM PLANNER

Every successful continuing education program has a "champion," someone who is deeply committed to making it happen. If you are the one responsible for leading and managing the development and planning process through these phases, you will play a variety of different roles all the time and take on a number of activities. In practice, role shifts will occur constantly and these roles and activities will blend together. This is surely challenging, but exciting and very rewarding if you develop a program that is a valuable educational experience.

Boyle (1981) identified four major roles for the continuing education programmer: (a) analyst, (b) stimulator, (c) facilitator, and (d) encourager. The analyst role begins with analyzing data collected and determining needs through the entire planning process. Each step and decision requires a diagnosis of the available options. Keeping the planning process going is the main function of the stimulator. In this role, the planner maintains the motivation and commitment to the program of all parties involved.

The facilitator must bring together the various players and resources to make the planning process work. The program planner creates an environment that will enable steady progress toward the goals of the program. Finally, the encourager eases tension, smooths over rough patches, and develops trust among the players. The encourager can help the players realize their goals by fostering individual and group potential.

Bear in mind that as the program planner you may not be the legitimate authority in decision making (Dahl, 1993). This role may belong to cosponsors, or even superiors in your own organization. You must seek out these decision makers. You may be held responsible for your products, but must use your leadership skills to coax support from these decision makers and to control the planning process. For that reason, we have added a fifth role, negotiator. Although negotiation is a part of the other four roles, the planner must be effective in creating conditions and options agreeable to all those involved.

The planner must work constantly for compromise and exhibit a great deal of diplomacy and tact when working with those whose opinions may differ substantially. Cervero and Wilson (1994) argue that negotiation describes what planners actually do and suggest negotiating interests as a model for planning practice.

We have already mentioned that you may be operating in a hostile environment with conflicting interests competing for a place for their vision for the program. Conflict is a natural phenomenon and can be both functional and dysfunctional (Trusty, 1987). You will have to manage the conflict to minimize the dysfunctional aspects and to maximize the positive aspects that conflict can generate in the planning process. Planning takes place in a particular institutional, political, and social context, and diplomacy is vital to the successful marriage of individual interests.

A sixth role then is that of communicator. As you go about the planning process and the presentation of the program, you will be constantly communicating information between those you are working with, cosponsors and participants. For example, you must communicate the goals of the program, the financial aspects of the program through a budget, and the results of the program through an evaluation. Keep people informed and be a good listener. Communication is a two-way process.

We cannot stress enough the importance of keeping the lines of communications open. It is vital to the success of the program that all participants know their duties and roles in the process. Showing that you respect them by keeping them informed of all aspects of the program will increase their level of commitment. Also, you are responsible for communicating to others the goals of your organization and its philosophy. This is communicated by your actions and as well as your words.

The role of the program planner can be likened to that of the "plate spinner" at the circus. You can have a number of "plates" spinning simultaneously. You can leave some of them alone for a short time while concentrating on the one at hand, but must keep returning to the others to maintain their momentum. We cannot tell you what to do in every situation, because each is unique. A theoretical knowledge base will help you make some sense of the situation. You must use your intuition, which is molded by time and experience gained with each program.

THE KNOWLEDGE AND SKILLS A PLANNER MUST POSSESS

In the roles you play as program planner and leader of the planning process, there are many tasks which you must complete. For this you will rely on the broad body of knowledge and skills which you learn both in formal learning settings and from practical experience. As you read this book, you will learn more about the knowledge and skills a planner must possess. These include a knowledge of how and why adults learn, and how to set objectives and choose appropriate learning activities. In addition you will need evaluation skills, budgeting and marketing skills, personal and communication skills. Managing the numerous details associated with conducting a continuing education program is another required ability.

An important foundation for building knowledge and skills is a personal philosophy that guides your actions and decisions. Guiding action is a strong sense of what is appropriate professional conduct. Experienced planners have emphasized the respect they have for participants and faith in their ability and willingness to learn. They express a similar respect for those with whom they work and are proud of the contribution that the educational programs they plan make to participants.

To support the individual knowledge and skills, the program planner should draw on the strengths of the organization, cosponsors, and those with whom they work. A significant strength is the experience, skills, and support that the administrative personnel can offer the planner. This support includes access to databases, computer and technical expertise, and contacts with community organizations.

LEADERSHIP

Continuing education programs are events often out of the routine for most people, and a program "champion" is needed to sustain commitment throughout all phases of program planning and operation. Bennis and Nanus (1985) identified four important factors that leaders must focus on to be effective in what they do:

1. Create focus and gain attention through vision.

2. Create meaning and identity through communication.

3. Develop trust and credibility.

4. Develop a self-image and an understanding of their own strengths and weaknesses.

Ideally, leadership should not rest in one person, but in a number of champions, each complementing the other.

Meister and Evers' (1985) study of the relationship between leadership and program development supports the need for strong, committed leaders who have a vision of what they intend to accomplish and who communicate that vision to colleagues. Their study also emphasizes how much a high level of commitment contributes to an effective planning process. In their words, leaders "give themselves to accomplishing their intentions and motivate others to do the same" (p. 1).

The leader is involved in many activities and has to play several roles simultaneously: that of visionary, shrewd analyst, effective money manager, well-organized controller of details, realist, diplomatic prodder, tough decision-maker, and cheerleader. Perhaps as important as all of these roles, the leader must understand the importance of information and keeping others informed. The leader must also bear in mind the educator's role. The program is designed to achieve certain specific educational goals. In the midst of many other financial and administrative matters, it is sometimes easy to forget that point.

SUMMARY

We have presented a five-phase approach to program development and the roles that program planners play as they take an idea, develop a concept for a program, and see it through to its delivery and wrap-up. As we have already stated, what may appear as a linear planning process, is not linear in practice. The boundaries between each phase are very fluid, and you will find yourself moving in and about each of the phases right to the conclusion of the entire planning process.

We have stated that you may substantially skip one or two of the phases. We caution, however, that judging the potential success of a program based solely on past success can be hazardous. Finally, you must understand your many roles and build the knowledge and skills necessary to perform them.

CHAPTER 2

Managing Challenges to Effective Planning

Planning continuing education programs presents a number of challenges. These challenges will arise as you move through the planning process, beginning immediately with the development of a clear concept for the program. They will not end until the completed program has been delivered, evaluated and reported upon, and offering it again is being discussed. These challenges will arise in different ways and at different times for each program, but all must be dealt with to move the program toward a successful completion.

In this chapter we discuss ten of the most common challenges you are likely to face. Each program is unique, and each will have its own set of challenges. Don't be looking for every challenge discussed here to appear in every program, and do not accept that these are the only challenges you will face.

DEVELOPING AND MAINTAINING A CLEAR PROGRAM CONCEPT

Developing and maintaining a clear concept for the program is a challenge that must be met before any effective steps can be taken in the planning process. The program concept will initially be developed through the idea generation phase as you begin to focus in on particular areas of concern, and topics designed to address them.

Creating a clear program concept is achieved by having a shared vision, that is a commonality of purpose and commitment by all those involved with the program. This is not an easy task, as you may be dealing with a number of cosponsors who have a personal vision for the program. Reaching a compromise may be difficult, sometimes impossible.

Just as important as developing the concept is the maintenance of that concept. That is not to say that the concept is so rigid as to not be open to a certain amount of subtle massaging and refinement. Shaping and reshaping may be necessary.

However, it is often the dramatic departure from the initial concept that leads a program to an unsuccessful conclusion. During the major planning phases, there could be a major departure from the concept; then perhaps you should consider this as an entirely new program and abandon your original idea as one that will not work. You actually start over, with new cosponsors, will have to spend time doing background research, and will begin the planning process again.

The program concept can be broad but should focus in on basic elements of the program. Is it a totally new program, a repeat of past efforts, or some modification of what has been done before? Who will attend and why would they be motivated to participate? Will participants be attending voluntarily or will there be some requirement, such as a certification mandate or the direction by a supervisor?

Examine what topics must be covered and why they are necessary for the program's success. Do they deal with information issues? Will they enable participants to increase their knowledge base in areas of importance to professional practice? Will some attempt be made to build necessary skills? What program format and learning activities will be most effective for delivering the subject matter?

Attention to the program's flow is the next item to be included. How much will be attempted in the time available? How many activities will be included, as well as recreation, entertainment, and exhibits. Be aware of the impression that this mix of educational and recreational activities will give. As the concept is shaped, consider some potential problems that you may face as the program is developed, planned, and operated, and make note of these. Past experience provides some guidance; so does your sense of the chemistry and agreement among the group planning the program.

We have included as Appendix A a sample planning interview worksheet that can be adapted and expanded to suit your own needs and the type of program being planned. The worksheet could be used to gather information to help develop the basic concept. Ask these questions of yourself, or of those who have contracted you to plan the program.

FINDING AND KEEPING COSPONSORS

Today, to a very great extent, continuing education programs must be sponsored by a variety of organizations. Often getting the sponsors is the easy part. Satisfying their demands while maintaining the educational focus of the program can be the real challenge. Sponsors are generally from one of six groups: (a) associations or professional societies sponsoring programs for their members; (b) corporations that provide programs for their employees, clients and customers, distribution agents, or shareholders; (c) not-for-profit agencies and public authorities or for-profit groups, all of which may be promoting a product, service or new concept for a community; (d) those who wish to be associated with a program because they share a similar philosophy, or who see future benefits accruing from such an association; (e) those who simply provide resources in return for self-promotion; and (f) those who offer conferences, seminars, workshops, and training sessions as a for-profit enterprise.

Financial considerations, resources that sponsors can contribute, and the part that sponsors can play in marketing a program are important reasons to expand involvement. Resources might include mailing lists, facilities, speakers, and written materials. Sponsors also can contribute valuable perspectives on various aspects of the program, bring experience to the planning, and help to evaluate what has been accomplished.

As you establish the program's foundation, a major task is to decide what the sponsorship arrangement will be. You will have to determine:

- Whether to have one or more major cosponsors and their identity
- What contributions they are expected to make

- What they expect to gain from involvement in the program
- What their instructional expectations are and what their fit is with the program's educational objectives and entertainment aspects
- Who secondary sponsors will be and what they will contribute

Answers to these questions will enable you to develop an overall approach to how the program will be developed and managed. You can then build a basic concept for the program and goals that all of the sponsors can accept and support. This is necessary for group ownership of the program to develop. The cosponsors' responses to the basic concept and the goals will tell you what will be required to maintain the relationships, how much involvement and assistance can be expected from them, and what problems you may have to face.

At this point, it is important you examine the mission or purpose of the cosponsoring organizations. You should consider what they do, their motivation for sponsorship, and why involvement with this program will contribute to what they are doing and their image. Are they involved in continuing education for profit, for self-promotion, to identify future opportunities, or as a part of their philosophy supporting continuing education? Do they have a commitment to affirmative action and a respect for diversity?

The motives of cosponsors should be carefully examined. If they are not clear, problems can occur at critical points in the planning process, when conflicting agendas of cosponsors create substantial discord, even a stalemate. Association with an inappropriate cosponsor can have a lasting effect on the program image and the image of other cosponsors.

As you look at brochures announcing various programs, you will see that cosponsorship brings together what may appear to be unusual combinations of cosponsors. If these are long-standing relationships with a history of successful programs, agreements have been reached about who does what and what is gained from continuing collaboration. In the beginning of the relationship, be sure to discuss what might be gained from cooperating. And later, you should regularly monitor the relationship to be sure that problems are both anticipated and addressed.

A useful body of research has been done on cosponsorship. Donaldson (1990), among others (Beder, 1984; Cervero, 1988; Dahl, 1993), has identified some of the gains possible through interorganizational cooperation. They include an increased ability to compete; the comfort in being able to share financial risk; the prestige gained through association with prestigious groups; a strengthened program, one able to attract more financial support; and an ability to withstand difficult times.

Some limitations identified include: the amount of extra time needed to work with one or more cosponsors; the loss of autonomy when decisions have to be approved by a group; the amount of compromise needed as a program is planned and operated; the challenge of reaching agreements, especially in financial areas; and the burden of keeping everyone informed. Above all, groups that work together may well have to give up some of their unique goals in favor of those of the temporary organization created to plan and operate programs.

In the role of facilitator, you must bring together the various players and resources to make the planning process work. Fragile coalitions may develop, and it is often a challenge to balance the input of the various groups so as to maintain harmony. However, you may forge very effective coalitions which lead to ongoing successful programs.

MAINTAINING COMMITMENT TO THE PLANNING PROCESS

As the planning proceeds, one of the daunting challenges is to maintain the commitment of all involved up to and including the program. This one program is not the sole activity in the day-to-day routine of all the planners. Time is a scarce commodity, and everyone is constantly trying to allocate valuable resources among many activities. Some will see this program as less important than others and so will need to be reminded of their commitment. Maintaining commitment is especially important when volunteers play a major role in the planning process and as the program is occurring.

An effective way of maintaining commitment is to establish

that shared vision mentioned earlier. By developing a shared vision, those involved will provide focus and energy because they are involved in something which matters to them. Involving potential participants in the planning also fosters commitment to the program. Perhaps the most important way of maintaining commitment is to keep communication channels open. Make sure that all those involved in planning and whose support is needed are kept informed of plans, problems, and progress. People do not want to be left out of the loop, nor do they want to be surprised by unannounced changes in direction or details.

MANAGING THE FINANCIAL RISK

Assuming the financial risk involved in program planning is a challenge that many people take on with little, if any, financial training or experience. As you will read in Chapter 6, having a clear concept for the program and sound objectives are an initial step in determining the cost of running the program and making sound decisions on the financial risk involved. There are often a number of people involved in the program who have a financial stake in it. Not only the cosponsors, but the participants may have made a commitment to the program both in time and in potential earnings forgone to participate in the program.

The financial risk is often greatest for new programs which may not have an established audience. There must be agreement between the cosponsors as to how the risk will be addressed and shared. Financial considerations have on occasion forced uncomfortable collaborations which can lead to further challenges.

RESOLVING CONFLICT

If your program has more than one cosponsor, politics will be a factor. Cosponsors come from different organizations with missions that vary, and their reasons for being involved in the program could vary and be unusual. Obtaining agreement could be very hard. Conflicts can occur over the basic purposes of the program. Sometimes potential cosponsors part company here.

There can be arguments over the number of participants who will attend, the registration fee, how much free time to allow, and when to start and end the program. And, perhaps, that is just the start of potential conflict. Constant compromises may be required.

In the role of negotiator you must create conditions and options agreeable to all those involved. That is a challenging mediation role. Managing conflict is a very real challenge in a time when divergent interests pursue their vision for the program, and where scarce resources can dictate who may appear to have the power in a particular situation.

You may find that, in the early stages of planning and establishing the program concept, there is a healthy working relationship between everyone. However, as time progresses and the program details become more concrete, people will discover that their differences in perspective are greater than first thought.

KEEPING PROGRAMS RELEVANT
AND COMPETITIVE

Planning continuing education programs occurs in an environment which is always changing. New knowledge and technology need to be communicated to various audiences, societal issues and norms fluctuate creating new forums for debate, changing work and leisure habits increase demands for new educational opportunities, and sources of funding and other support diminish. These changes are beyond the control of the program planner and present the challenge of being prepared to respond to new demands.

Keeping programs relevant is an important function which can be overlooked where programs have been operating for an extended period. A long-running program may fail, not because of its basic design but because it no longer serves the audience for which it was developed (Broomall & Skwarek, 1991). Planners can lose touch with participants and feel they know what topics should be covered. That is often a fatal assumption.

Each time the program is to be offered, you should question its objectives and content and the cost/benefit relationship.

Has the program retained its distinctiveness? There is little to be gained from preserving a program past its worth at the expense of new, innovative and relevant directions. Staying in touch with participants, being knowledgeable about the content addressed, and consulting experts are ways to address this challenge. Knowing your competitors and what programs they are offering will also help you remain relevant and competitive.

MANAGING THE DETAILS OF PROGRAM PLANNING

As you begin to read Chapter 6, you may be awed by the countless details which must be attended to as the program starts to become a reality and then as you see it to its conclusion. Depending on the size of the program there will be many individuals involved in numerous tasks. Keeping track of all these people and the many details assigned to them requires good planning and organization. The one thing you will soon discover about program planning is the level of unpredictability.

Unimagined and unforeseen events occur that can create chaos and may demand significant changes in the program. The key to meeting this challenge is being prepared for the unexpected. Through experience and a certain amount of intuition, you will begin to develop contingency plans for many of the problem that may arise.

MEASURING SUCCESS AND FAILURE, AND DEALING WITH IT

A program may be considered successful for many reasons. Planners should reach early agreement on how success will be determined. The criteria you choose will help identify what you want to know about the planning process and the program and the information you will need to gather. Lewis and Dunlop (1991) fault those who consider the number of participants as the sole criterion for defining success. Through their interviews with practitioners, these researchers identified a mix of quantitative and qualitative factors that can be used to assess success, including:

1. High demand for the program

2. Participant satisfaction

3. Increased visibility, credibility, and good will in the community

4. High level of participant involvement and interest

5. Meeting financial objectives

Orem and Brue (1991) in a survey of providers of continuing professional education identify a number of predictors of program success including:

1. Accurate assessment of learners' needs

2. Quality of program design and delivery

3. Critical timing in delivery of pertinent topic

4. Support from stakeholders

The measures suggested mean that a program having fewer participants than the budget break-even number can, in fact, be considered a success. Other goals may have been reached including, for example, the development of important relationships that may lead to future programs. The use of program objectives as the sole criterion for appraising success is also inappropriate. There are unintended outcomes that did not figure into our goal-setting exercise.

It is important that you have the opportunity to add new success criteria and alter existing criteria during the planning process. All those involved in planning the program should have an opportunity to identify their own criteria. The evaluation can then produce data that you can use to determine the level of success and where the program fell short.

Finally, are you willing to accept failure? The very real challenge in evaluating program success is accepting that all of your efforts produce very little in a way of positive outcomes. But remember, your criteria for success may be different from those of others, and even though you may see the program as a failure others may consider it a success.

CHOOSING THE RIGHT PROGRAM FORMAT AND APPROPRIATE LEARNING ACTIVITIES

Choosing the format in which to present the program content is sometimes self-evident as, for example, a conference for the annual meeting of a professional association. But this is not always the case. The choice of format can have a significant impact on the effectiveness of the program and should be appropriate to the content and the audience. The decision on format will be made as part of the basic concept and will convey to the potential participants what they can generally expect in the way of information delivery and the degree of participation and interaction. For example, a program in art appreciation might be best served by a visit to an art museum supported by appropriate commentary.

There is a broad range of program formats and more than one format may be combined to present a program. Within these program formats a variety of individual learning activities may be used to delivery the content. Learning activities are discussed in Chapter 4. Some learning activities create a passive learning environment and others are more active. Participants come with preferred learning styles, and you must both know them and decide to what extent you can depart from them.

Moss (1989) provides an excellent summary of most program formats in which he discusses uses, advantages, and limitations for each format as well as the facilities required and procedures for use and some very useful hints. For further readings on program formats we suggest Apps (1991), Caffarella (1988), and Knox (1990). Also see Appendix B.

The challenge is finding the appropriate mix of learning activities which complement the format and present the content in a manner which maximizes learning. You also have to consider how much participants expect to be entertained while they learn or instead of learning. Battles occur here, as reality and the desire to provide a rigorous educational program conflict.

MAKING PROGRAMS ACCESSIBLE TO PARTICIPANTS

There are many reasons why individuals attend programs. The challenge is to make programs accessible to all those who want to attend and assist them in overcoming any obstacles to participation. Those obstacles can be classified under three headings: (a) situational barriers, which arise simply because the individual's current life situation; (b) institutional barriers, which present practical obstacles to participation; and (c) dispositional barriers, which relate to attitude and personal beliefs about learning (Cross, 1981).

By evaluating the potential group of participants and the cosponsors, ways to overcome those barriers might be identified. Registration fees might be subsidized by a cosponsor. The length of the program could be reduced, lowering the registration fee and making it possible for others to attend. A more accessible location could be chosen. Topics could be presented in a way that makes them more attractive to reluctant learners.

Marketing material is another way participants can be made to feel welcome. Explanations of who should attend and what will be gained are ways of encouraging further participation.

Another way of making programs accessible is to consider the status of your program. By status we mean its position or its rank in importance among similar programs, other educational opportunities, even other day-to-day activities and basic must-do tasks of potential participants. They prioritize activities and opportunities when deciding what they can fit into their busy schedules. Not only do potential participants prioritize opportunities, but so do potential cosponsors and other groups such as employers and government agencies who may support participation by their staff. The factors that help determine program status are viewed differently by each of these groups.

Internal and external factors are considered when prioritizing activities and opportunities. Internal factors include barriers to participation, relevance and appropriateness of the program, setting, sponsor reputation, and respect for tradition and diversity. These issues may also be viewed as external factors. Other external factors include the program objectives, structure, size and length, cost of participation, associated activities, and status of resource persons.

Hundreds of programs are offered every day. Why does someone stop and read a brochure? Basically it is a sense of gain that outweighs the real and perceived barriers. This means that the potential participant gives the program high status because of a number of factors including the program of events and format, what information will be presented, who will be speaking, where it will be held, who the other participants will be, the cosponsors, and value for money. The challenge is how to raise the status of the program so that attending becomes a priority to a sufficient number of individuals.

Not only is it a challenge to make programs accessible, but you may also be dealing with those who are not enthusiastic about participating. They may be attending for a number of reasons, not of their own choosing. Dealing with these negative attitudes is a challenge, and although you may not be able to affect negative attitudes, you will need to work at preventing them from affecting other participants.

SUMMARY

We have brought attention to some of the many challenges to be met in program planning. There is no complete list. Perhaps the challenge which we failed to address was the challenge for knowing that other obstacles and opportunities will arise and the challenge of being confident in meeting those unforeseen challenges.

As you confront and deal with these challenges, remember that not only are you moving the program toward a successful conclusion, but that you are learning many lessons for yourself and about yourself. You are building your experiences into a rich body of practical knowledge about how adults learn and develop, how organizations operate and develop, how people function in what are often chaotic situations, and how best to plan continuing education programs. You are also developing personal philosophies about adult and continuing education and program development and planning which will guide your approach to future planning.

LIBRARY
College of St. Francis
JOLIET, ILLINOIS

157,437

CHAPTER 3

Building a Foundation for Success

Today, more than ever, sound planning is a must. Competition has increased substantially. Participants are much more frugal about the money they will allocate to continuing education activities. A great deal of money has to be spent before a program takes place, sums that may never be recovered. The image of a sponsor can be diminished if a program has to be canceled or is offered with less than anticipated results.

A solid foundation for planning is the development of a clear concept for the program, and based on information gathered you can determine if a decision to go ahead is appropriate. As you develop the concept, think a great deal about why a program is being held, who might attend, and why.

From the outset, and continuing through the process to the completion of the program, you will be gathering information. The effective program developer will be like a sponge, absorbing information from a variety of sources. After sorting and analyzing the information you collect, you will have to make decisions as to the direction you will take with the planning process. This will require you to prioritize your options before choosing those that work best in the current context and make your decision to proceed or to abandon the program.

In this chapter we will consider why programs are offered and who might participate and why. Then we will look at sources of information and their value, consider how to sort through the information and make informed choices among the available options based on the criteria you have established, and finally, you will begin to see how your planning brings you to the point where you will decide whether or not to commit to the program, the go/no-go decision.

WHY PROGRAMS ARE OFFERED AND WHO ATTENDS

Each program is held for specific reasons. Generally programs can be categorized as being informational, skill or competence building, or adding to existing knowledge. The reasons for participation are as infinite as the reasons for offering the program. Consider both the educational and noneducational reasons which motivate participation.

Potential participants may have an interest in personal or professional improvement, but other reasons for their attendance may be as significant or more influential than the educational content when making a decision to attend a program. People are motivated to accomplish specific goals or gain particular knowledge or skills, to interact with others, to respond to peer or career pressures including professional requirements, or to gain personal improvement and fulfillment through both the educational and recreational aspects.

SOURCES OF INFORMATION

There are five basic sources of information that can be examined and used in making a decision to proceed. The first is past experience with the planned or similar programs, and what that experience provides as guidance. Second is background information that will identify trends and educational interests the proposed program can address. The third source of information is knowledge of what the competition is doing, increasingly important today in a crowded continuing education marketplace. Fourth, you can take advice from a variety of sources; through that advice, in combination with the other information, sound decisions can be made about whether or not to proceed. Finally, look at the "numbers," that is, a preliminary budget and an estimate of the number of participants.

Past Experience

Through past experience, a program developer can look at the success potential of a program and make realistic assessments of how many participants can be expected. Past experience will also identify necessary levels of support, including such things as cosponsorship and financial assistance needed.

Often overlooked but of great value are evaluations of past programs, which tell you what participants liked and disliked. These evaluations can be of the program if it is to be repeated, of course. If you have information collected from participants about somewhat comparable programs, this can tell you what those participants would expect in future programs including program length, necessary amenities, learning activities, and registration fees. But remember, these are often different participants and the past is just a guide, not a rule.

Past experience can be a guide in additional ways. You should review notes, planning interview worksheets, memos, meeting summaries, and your own recollections associated with cosponsors. The difficult or ease of working with one or more organizations and the individuals representing them should be clear to you. For example, what approvals will be necessary to obtain financial support or a mailing list? Who will make the decisions?

You can also learn how many participants can realistically be expected and what their registration pattern has been in the past. Will one mailing be sufficient, or will a number of reminders be necessary? How sophisticated must the marketing material be? Can you send a letter, or will a very attractive and colorful brochure be needed? This information should be considered in your marketing plan.

Some participants, those in large government agencies or corporations, may need to get approval from a number of managers, and that may slow down registration. Instead of panicking, you may know that 25 percent or more of the registrations will come in at the last minute. There may even be a significant percentage of walk-ins, those participants who don't advance register. Include this sort of information in your planning and registration time line if it is appropriate.

Past experience, above all, should focus your attention on the problems that can occur. Anything and everything can go wrong, from site managers losing a contract, to weather problems delaying participants' registration, to necessary material not arriving on time. Throughout the planning, and especially the early planning, you should keep reviewing these problems. Sometimes you just anticipate them; on other occasions, you may decide that the struggles are too great, given what can be expected from this program, and canceling it is the wisest course of action.

You should take all of the necessary time to think through past experiences. This review is more effective when a group does it rather than an individual. Once a list is made, look it over carefully and ask if any useful piece of information has been forgotten. That list also should be reviewed while the program is in planning stages and even during its operation. As the philosopher George Santayana said so many years ago, "Those who don't study the past are cursed to repeat it."

Background and Trend Information

One of the icons of continuing education program development has been a needs assessment of what participants may want. On some occasions, gathering that information will be a valuable contribution to the development process and to a sound decision to go ahead or not.

As literature on needs assessment points out, data gathering will of necessity take time. A survey instrument will have to be developed and refined, and then tested. That survey must go to those who will respond; reminders may have to be sent to get a sufficient response. The information will have to be coded and then analyzed. Finally, a report will have to be written.

If these steps don't daunt you, consider another problem. Data from those who respond to a survey indicating what may interest them enough to participate isn't always reliable. What looks interesting as a potential program topic on a survey may not translate into a strong programming idea and may result in low registration.

Other kinds of background research can identify factors that may lead a very clearly defined audience to your program. An important question you should seek to answer is, "What is happening that will motivate participants to attend a program?" The happenings could include:

1. Changes in laws that affect their practice

2. New technology that will make them more competitive or less susceptible to litigation

3. Research that shows them methods to improve practice

4. Events in the next town, another part of the country, or internationally that could affect the way they do business

5. The emergence of a figure whose views are particularly insightful or helpful

The term used to describe gathering information like this is environmental scanning, and those who have products and services to sell have been doing it long before it was recognized in continuing education. Before that, the intelligence community used the process to assemble discrete pieces of information into a mosaic that tells a story. That is what planners whose programs set the standard seem to do.

Simpson, McGinty, and Morrison (1987) describe the process as the systematic collection of information. As opposed to randomly collecting items, there is a regular flow of material and discussion of implications for action. Specific publications and other sources of reliable information are checked regularly. Through this process, trends are identified and ideas for programs rapidly explored. Response is rapid and appropriate.

Through this scanning, for example, those who provide continuing professional education programs to the staff of hospitals and clinics may notice how the health professions are becoming sensitive to customer service and as a result, develop programs for care givers. The staff of a community college continuing education unit in a large city completed a study which found that young single professionals saw educational programs as an excellent way to meet others without consuming alcohol in smokey taverns and clubs.

As part of the development and planning process this information can contribute to productive discussion on what programs might be effective and worth pursuing. Ideas can be considered and then quickly discarded. Planning that relies on useful information becomes part of the routine. The important point here is that the decisions made are informed decisions.

The Competition

Competition is an asset to program planning. It challenges us to improve the quality of our programs, and it also makes us pay careful attention to the market and where we fit in that market. As you evaluate the competition, be concerned not only with what they are doing but with the hold they may have on the market they serve. Important information can be gathered through an assessment of the competition that reveals how much of a challenge it will be to enter this market. Consider the following aspects of competition, as you assess the ability of a new program to compete.

1. The strength of their marketing and your ability to match it to reach the same population

2. The length of time that they have been offering the program which you now want to present, and the features you propose that will make your program more attractive

3. The broad goal of their program and how it may differ in terms of an emphasis on education or recreation and entertainment

4. Their image and how it may make you seem like an interloper or an incompetent substitute

5. Their facilities or locations and your ability to match them

6. A comparison between their registration fees and yours

Answers to these questions will help you decide if the risk is a sensible one. We don't mean to be discouraging but to strongly suggest realism. Still, your thorough analysis may reveal certain problems with the competition, and careful thought may produce ways to improve upon their efforts, enabling you to grab a share of the market.

You should have a continuing supply of material from your competition, immediate and national. Read their brochures carefully to see what they offer, especially anything that is unique. Newspaper advertisements are another important source of useful comparative information. You also can learn from presentations made at conferences and other programs you attend as a participant.

When you combine environmental scanning with a review of the competition, your assessment of where you stand in the continuing education market becomes a better one. Discussion can include determining the extent to which you can compete and what can be learned from others who do what you do.

Advice from Others

Effective program developers listen a great deal and have developed a network of individuals that can be consulted in various ways. Both formal and informal means should be used. We cannot rely entirely on statistics, demographics, and our individual past experience to plan programs. Community representatives should be an integral part of committees providing advice (Charuhas, 1993). These people can help interpret the figures, expand the concept of continuing education to others, and bring more participants to what will be a more meaningful program.

We strongly suggest that you define "advice" in the broadest possible terms. By doing so, you have an opportunity to be flexible and rely on both individuals and groups in a number of different committee formats and sizes. For example, you can call on colleagues for advice or invite a group of potential participants to informally discuss ideas or constitute a formal committee. There are a number of approaches available to gather advice.

Depending upon the type of program, you may be required to have a formal planning or advisory committee. Traditions of program management or rules governing how a particular program operates will mandate the number of people and the representation needed. In certain contexts, participation by members of the intended audience is very important and strongly advocated. In fact, the intended audience may drive the whole planning process, using you as a facilitator and resource person.

Valuable guidelines for your consideration have been developed by those with extensive experience with committee formation and use (Boyle, 1981; Dahl, 1993; Kozoll, 1980) and include:

1. Knowing the purpose the committee will serve and defining its boundaries of operation and authority of members

2. Careful selection of those who will serve according to the contributions they can make

3. Being realistic about the members' willingness and ability to contribute

4. Setting a time limit for members' involvement

Nadler and Nadler (1987) introduce a potentially useful term in their material on the role of committees. They stress the design function these groups perform and how input from a comprehensive group can improve the overall quality of any program. Members of a well-selected advisory or planning committee can bring additional elements to the process, and reflect on the importance of information as important decisions are made.

The literature that supports the value of planning or advisory committees is very positive. Careful planners should, however, consider some potential problems these groups can create:

1. Personalities may not blend, and meetings could be filled with arguments, rather than productive work. A need for control by one or more members could further limit committee output.

2. The most appropriate people needed to form a truly effective and valuable committee may not have the time to provide the assistance required. For example, they may come unprepared for a meeting, not having read information that will be discussed.

3. Personal agendas may be very important to individual members. Agendas could include fundamentals such as the direction the program should take. Conflict may be a problem from the start.

Committee advice and direction can be valuable, but you must be very aware ahead of time of the risks involved. The committee must be organized and focused to contribute to the planning of a program. It should not create another problem you will have to address.

Another source of advice is an *ad hoc* group brought together for as long as you need their input. This type of group, not unlike focus groups used in marketing research, could come together once and never again. A clear agenda must be stressed in charging an *ad hoc* committee. You are more likely to be able to call upon these individuals again if you make sound use of their time. And, of course, if you can show them just how much their advice has made a difference to the program, their willingness to contribute will grow even more.

Advice from a network of trusted contacts and colleagues is always beneficial and, depending upon the type of program and your experience with it, may be all the advice you need. You may have just a few questions, perhaps about a potential speaker or a site to be used. Phone calls or a brief meeting will give you the answers you need.

Today, large and small businesses have become far more sensitive to their customers and are using focus groups to obtain information from them. A review of the literature on the process of using these groups (Byers & Wilcox, 1991; Kruger, 1988; O'-Donnell, 1988) reveals that many of the same elements in forming an effective advisory committee are used in a focus group. Especially important is planning the meetings and questions that will be used to obtain information from a group of individuals.

Those questions have to be very specific and designed to get answers to questions of importance to planning a program.

The person who leads those focus groups sessions is very important and should be selected with great care. Skillful individuals can obtain a lot of valuable information in a short time. They are able to ask good questions and summarize, yet refrain from adding their opinions. Information obtained from focus groups should be summarized quickly, with trends and significant ideas identified. The writings cited earlier advise caution in generalizing from what those in a focus group have contributed. Their ideas should be blended with other information.

Finally, constructive criticism is a form of advice sometimes forgotten. It sometimes appears without your asking for it. Constructive critics who can ask difficult questions are valuable people. They include those with some knowledge of program planning, but who may not have direct knowledge of your particular program. They are not out to sabotage your program. Often they can save you much time, expense, and personal grief. Their questions may, for example, help you recognize a simple oversight or potential cost overruns, force you to revise your projections of participation, or cause you to reconsider the implicit objectives for offering the program. The person to whom you report could be such a critic, as are colleagues planning other programs.

As the program planning process proceeds, you may need to use different groups, even different types and structures of groups and different forms of advice for different elements of the planning process. You may need to draw on specialists in different fields at various times to provide input and to strengthen the decision-making process.

The Numbers

Even though most continuing educators would prefer not to think of the financial implications of developing and presenting a program, it is usually the bottom line, or the financial numbers, which has a significant influence on the decision to proceed or not. The development of a preliminary budget is the final source of valuable information that can contribute to your decision.

Will the numbers work when you do an initial budget? They should work in different ways. First, income should at least equal and preferably exceed expenses. Second, the registration fee should be consistent with the amounts participants are prepared to pay. Third, you should be able to recover costs with the lowest possible number of participants. If you feel that 100 people will register, build a budget with a break-even point of 50 registrations. Finally, inflate expenses, especially those related to marketing, and include a miscellaneous line in the budget that is at least equal to five percent of the fixed cost component.

You will be able to budget more confidently with a program with past success. A new program breaking into a new market carries a greater risk, and the budget should be approached with conservatism and caution.

As you develop a preliminary budget prior to making a decision to go ahead or to cancel the program, consider the following questions:

1. How much marketing will have to be done, and to whom, to obtain the break-even number of registrants? At what cost?

2. Who will speak or present? What will their participation cost?

3. How much staff time will be involved and at what cost?

4. Where will the program be held and at what cost?

5. What meal functions must be held, and what will they cost?

6. Will any special equipment be needed, and what will it cost to rent? Will operators be required and at what cost?

7. What materials will be provided to participants, and what will they cost?

8. Will any special staff be needed to assist with the program? How much will their wages amount to?

9. Can we expect any other miscellaneous expenses?

10. How many participants will be needed to cover fixed expenses? What is the history of attendance at this program?

11. Is the registration fee within the limits of the intended audience?

SORTING OUT THE INFORMATION AND CREATING OPTIONS

All the information collected must be sorted and examined to determine if it makes sense to go ahead. You are assessing the extent of risk, and what you know will minimize that risk.

At this point, you should know the following:

1. The strength of the leadership and support for this program

2. The clarity of the concept for the program and the depth of commitment to making it a reality

3. The evident need for the program

4. The competition and how strong it is

5. What advisors have told you about the soundness of the idea

6. How realistic the budget is, given conservative attendance estimates

You can't attach numbers to what you know or use a formula that will indicate that going ahead is the most logical step to take. What you will be doing is weighing this information and making a somewhat subjective judgment about what are your priorities with this program. Boyle (1981) suggests that priorities are "what is important or valuable at the present time" (p. 178). The importance of the information you collect to assist in making a decision should be viewed in the organizational, political, and social context in which the planning is taking place.

For example, the budget may not be the most desirable but those involved in the planning feel that the program is important and should be held. By contrast, the budget could be solid but cosponsors are potentially incompatible. Your decision to proceed is important nonetheless.

Questions which may help you decide what decision to make include:

1. Will the program contribute to our collective image?

2. Will a particular group benefit from the information?

3. Will a community or an organization be affected positively?

4. Do we have the administrative structure to handle the details?

We have already indicated that planning programs is not for the faint of heart. Certainly some programs have a long and established history of success and there really is no decision needed; the program will take place. But in many other situations, past history, the best information and advice you can gather, and what your intuition tells you are the available tools to make this important decision.

PUTTING THE PIECES TOGETHER
AND MAKING INFORMED DECISIONS

The pieces of information you have collected should form a picture that either points to potential success, a clear risk, or definite failure. With that information, you are in a position to make a decision about your next steps. There may be an occasion where the information would lead you to cancel the program but you still feel that offering the program is a risk that should be taken. You take the risk and proceed because, for example, you desire to develop a new market or showcase some aspect of your organization. Not all decisions have to be completely rational ones! Calculated risks should be part of continuing education. Without them, there would be precious little growth and innovation.

Realism, of course, is necessary. Money and time will be expended, your image will be put on the line, and an entire temporary organization will have to be put in place, if a decision to go ahead is made. Questions must be asked and honest answers provided. The following may be useful questions to pose in all cases, and especially when the program is new.

1. Does our organization have a track record in this area and the necessary expertise to plan and run the program we have envisioned?

2. Is there a clearly identifiable audience, and is it one we can attract? Is it large enough to meet the minimum registration number?

3. What past successes can we build on, including the necessary administrative support structure?

4. Do we have access to the facilities that participants will expect?

5. Do we have access to the experts necessary to address the topics that have been identified?

6. Is there a group to whom we can turn for advice and who will champion the program? Do any represent organizations likely to provide us with financial support?

7. Do we have sufficient money to risk for marketing and other expenses that may not be recovered, even if the program is offered?

8. If we market the program and too few register, what will be the impact of cancellation? Will our image be harmed in any way?

9. How valid is the program content and is it a program we can offer more than once?

We do not mean to suggest that your decision to proceed or cancel should be based on economic reasons alone, although whatever your decision, there will certainly be a financial effect.

The initial stages of the planning process can be educational for those unfamiliar with the complexities of planning a continuing education program. Those with limited experience may have unrealistic expectations, such as the ease of attracting potential participants or how quickly details can be addressed. A budget planning exercise will bring some sense of reality to the planning process. It may show, for example, how much special events added to a program can quickly escalate costs.

The information gathered underlines the realities about the number of individuals likely to attend, the competition, and the costs involved. That information may be not what the planner wants to hear, but a sound decision has to be made, one based on reality rather than hope.

As you put together the pieces and have time to work with cosponsors and others involved with the program, you will begin to get a "feel" for the program. This is where you own intuition, experience, and common sense are valuable. You will begin to sense whether or not this program, even the whole planning structure which is unfolding, will be viable not only in economic terms but also philosophically. You may wish to consider some of these questions in reaching your decision:

- Can I really work effectively with the appointed planning committee, the cosponsors, and other stakeholders?
- Am I prepared to compromise sufficiently to accommodate the goals of others?
- Is the content of the program or its general theme something I wish to be associated with? Will my personal values conflict with the program goals?
- Am I prepared to accept the responsibility for such a program?

In some cases, what to do will be very evident and your decision to go ahead or cancel at this point will be very clear. More often, you will have to consider all the facts and your instincts very carefully and then make a decision with which you are still not fully comfortable.

SUMMARY

Gathering information and sorting through it carefully lead you to make an informed decision as to whether or not to proceed with the program. That information comes from many sources, sometimes unexpected sources. By scanning the environment to look at what has been done in the past, what others are doing, what seems to be popular, and what trends are developing, we begin to see where we fit in the continuing education environment. Taking advice from a number of sources that may be closer to the topic brings us nearer to what the potential participant wants in a program. Looking at preliminary numbers is essential in this stage of planning.

The planning which builds a foundation for success continues through the entire process until the completion of the program. Planning does not cease when the decision to commit to the program has been made. We are always collecting information, seeking advice, and checking the numbers, and at any time we may reach the point where it is time to abandon the program and accept the loss.

If at any time you make the decision not to proceed with the program, do not think that the planning is necessarily a failure. The decision was made after careful consideration of all aspects of the program, including the intended participants, sponsors, financial and other resources, and consideration of your own "comfort level." What you have done is made a very wise business decision. You have engaged in a market research exercise which has identified a sector of the market that is not an appropriate one for you at this time. As we have said before, the decision has been an informed decision.

CHAPTER 4

Planning for Success

Even when a decision to go ahead has been made, challenges will remain. Three are identified in the following brief examples:

- The planning committee provided the person in charge of the program with a draft schedule. Meal and break times and the social events had already been decided. "You can fill up the rest of the time with meetings and such," the program chair was told. A second message was that those events shouldn't get in the way of the truly important activities.
- "We want much more time to talk. This is one occasion when we can find out what our colleagues are doing. Make sure the breaks are long enough and we end early enough in the day to have time to talk!" This message on past evaluations was a very clear and consistent one.
- "There has to be a 'name' speaker," those on the planning committee were told. "And that person better be entertaining!" From that moment on, the entire focus of the planning committee's work was to find that 'name' and get a commitment from that speaker.

You may think you are planning a strictly educational program. As these examples indicate, you will have other considerations to address and you must give them the proper thought. These three examples also were included to suggest that educational intent may have to be shaped to fit into other motives for holding a program.

Planning the educational aspects of the program includes establishing both the explicit and implicit objectives that are to be achieved, identifying the most appropriate learning activities to satisfy those objectives, and determining who will make presentations and lead the learning activities. As soon as the decision to proceed has been made, you can turn your attention to the educational aspects of the program.

Even when the cosponsors of a program, or the participants themselves, emphasize social or entertainment dimensions, you have a responsibility to stress the value of the educational portions. You can do this by concentrating on packaging the educational aspects of the program in a way that is both attractive and relevant.

In this chapter, we provide a brief introduction to how adults learn, examine the development of objectives and appropriate learning activities, and discuss the selection of speakers and presenters. Developing objectives, their related learning activities, and who will present are very closely tied and are integral to the program's overall quality. Therefore, you need to pay close attention to these dimensions, and you should understand that a considerable amount of time is needed to develop them. An often neglected dimension of planning which is discussed in this chapter is the climate and setting in which the program takes place. As you begin to negotiate with presenters and site managers, you must be attentive to the legal issues which may arise in the course of planning and conducting the program. Some of these issues are addressed here. Finally we discuss continuous evaluation and how it can be used to improve the planning process and the program.

As we begin to explore in detail the development of the educational aspects of the program, we must clarify that you need to distinguish between setting objectives and developing associated learning activities that (a) have a broad focus on what is to be accomplished by the entire program, and (b) those which are more narrowly focused on individual learning activities.

As a planner you will first be concerned with program objectives and the format of learning activities. After these are established and you have chosen the appropriate persons to deliver the program content, you may need to work with those presenters to develop individual instructional objectives and learning activities that fit the program objectives and can be accommodated within the program format. The approach is much the same in both situations, although you will be dealing with greater specificity in developing individual learning activities. In this chapter we shall address them together.

HOW ADULTS LEARN

As a planner, you should be familiar with how and why adults learn and change. The literature on adult learning (Brookfield, 1986; Cross, 1981; Galbraith, 1991; Houle, 1961; Jarvis, 1987; Knox, 1990; Mezirow, 1991; Tennant, 1988; Tough, 1968, 1982) provides numerous theories of adult learning, provides a description of the characteristics of adults as learners, and presents a number of principles of adult learning. Merriam and Caffarella (1991) provide a comprehensive summary of these theories as four orientations to learning. Briefly, these four orientations are:

- Behaviorist. The focus of this orientation is the reinforcement of stimuli in the learning situation which are intended to change behavior.
- Cognitive. Theories focus on internal mental processes and how information is stored, retrieved, and used in the change process.
- Humanistic. Humanists believe that learning is guided by individual choice and responsibility and is affected by human nature and emotions.
- Social Learning. From this perspective, it is believed that learning is a function of the interaction of the individual, the environment, and behavior.

As a practitioner you can use your knowledge of adult learning to develop effective learning activities and to guide your search for solutions to problems that may arise in planning and conducting these learning activities. For example, you may be working with a planning committee that is familiar with very traditional learning activities; that is, a lecturer talks and participants listen, take notes, and ask respectful questions. You can and should suggest other approaches, especially those that involve the participants, increasing their feelings of mastery over the material being addressed and involvement in the learning process.

A second very important contribution you can make is to increase sensitivity to the different ways adults learn and why they learn. You can raise these two questions: "Will those attending this program be motivated to learn? Why?" Studies by Aslanian and Bricknell (1980) indicate that certain trigger events in the life of adults can increase motivation to learn and the willingness to concentrate on material presented at a program. A long list of those events can be written, including a lost job, a significant change in the technology affecting how work is done, or the need to better understand customers or clients. As learning activities are shaped, you should be looking for those trigger events as one way to better understand and serve program participants.

Boyle (1981) encourages program planners to take into account the past experiences of those participating. Those past experiences include how the participants expect to learn, how successful they have been in learning situations, and the depth or limits of experience. This last factor can increase or decrease a participant's ability to relate to the material being presented. Think for a moment about the challenges associated with discussing another culture with those whose travel has been limited or explaining advances in computers with those having only basic knowledge of this technology.

Along this same line of thinking, you may find that within a group there may be participants who are at different levels of familiarity with the material. You will have to determine the level at which you will pitch the program content so as not to alienate any of the participants. It may require a change in format, for example, to include discussion groups which can build on the differing knowledge or skill levels.

Feedback to learners on how they are doing is considered important. Adults look for confirmation and support of their learning. It must be determined when to provide feedback and in what form it will take. The feedback must also be relevant for the participants.

The concept of "transfer of learning" (Lauffer, 1978) suggests that consideration be given to how participants will apply what is learned. The question of "if" learning will be applied also must be addressed. Is it appropriate to provide information on a new procedure that can't be applied because the participant's employer is unlikely to accept it? Tallman and Holt (1987) suggest that most programmers fail to emphasize the transfer factor, focusing on delivery. They continue to say that if program planners are committed to the learning process and change, then they must pay more attention to what happens after the program is complete.

Lauffer also suggests that consideration be given to how much material can be retained and cities studies of how much is lost after participants leave an educational program. According to Lauffer, "Both retention and transfer are strengthened when learning occurs in a meaningful context" (p. 203). To Lauffer, this means active involvement where participants discuss or play roles. Experiential learning (Chickering, 1971; Kolb, 1984) considers the connection between experience and learning. By understanding this connection you can bring learning and reality closer. Learning exercises that build on experience can be valuable and help create the meaningful context referred to by Lauffer.

There also may be situations where participants can learn a great deal yet remain generally very passive. Video presentations of case examples bring real life into the room, as does the presence of people telling what they have learned and what participants should avoid doing. "Meaningful" can be defined in many ways.

A point that is often overlooked when objectives and learning activities are developed is that ideally, education should equip a participant to be more capable of finding other ways and places to continue to learn. Lauffer (1978) argues that the instructor, the environment where learning is to take place, and the learners themselves should encourage the "tilt" toward independence.

Finally, it is important to realize that adults learn in a variety of ways. Each individual has a preferred learning style. Apps (1991) categorizes adult learners into three learning styles: (a) intuitive, learners who like to be in control of their learning; (b) sequential, learners who appreciate structured learning; and (c) practical, those who want learning that has immediate application. Formal measures of preferred learning styles are available (Myers-Briggs Type Indicator, Kolbs Learning Style Inventory, the Canfield Learning Styles Inventory), and you may consider using these in developing individual learning activities.

However, many learners have as a learning preference the one particular method to which they have always been exposed (Apps, 1991). By providing a variety of learning activities you will cater to a diversity of learning styles if they exist among the participants. More importantly, you contribute to the maturing of the adult as a learner. Participants may in fact discover that they value other styles of learning and grow more confident as they engage in a variety of approaches.

PROGRAM OBJECTIVES

Goal statements are your road map. When they are well-stated, they provide your program with focus and direction (Caffarella, 1988). They establish benchmarks against which progress can be measured and the program evaluated. You can define the criteria for success so that it is more likely to be achieved. Objectives can motivate achievement.

Objectives will be on a continuum from general to specific. They should be (a) simple, (b) measurable, (c) achievable, and (d) consistent with the overall goal of the program. To this extent, Boyle (1981) advocates realism in setting objectives as a must. However, Houle (1972) makes the point that objectives cannot be completely comprehensive and will not account for all contingencies. With this in mind, you should be prepared to modify objectives as you proceed with the planning or the learning activity.

We believe that objectives are valuable for three other reasons:

1. They establish boundaries for the program and make it easier to identify the range of effort needed. The program's focus narrows, as one result, and the program's purpose and image

are clearer. Marketing material is more easily prepared and understood.

2. The proposed accomplishments are clearly communicated to those who might participate; they can identify what will be gained from attendance. That potential gain is important when managers or others to whom a potential participant reports must approve attendance.

3. You cannot assume that presenters understand the program's intent or even their part in it. Therefore objectives are an important orientation tool you can use to acquaint speakers and others who will make a contribution to the program. Time spent with these people can result in their making more relevant contributions, based on an understanding of their role in achieving the program objectives.

Objectives can be explicit, those which clearly state what is to be achieved, and implicit, those which are not readily apparent to the participant and are less directly related to the educational dimensions of the program. The objectives are complementary, and you may use the explicit objective to disguise the implicit objectives of the program. Implicit objectives are not meant to be covert, but represent subtle ways of achieving broad educational and organizational goals.

Explicit Objectives

Explicit objective statements are designed to make clear to potential participants exactly what can be expected. They communicate the focus of the program and become the guide used in identifying the kinds of learning activities that will be used. As mentioned earlier in this chapter, program evaluations can be constructed using these explicit objectives. Objectives also can be statements that clarify how the information to be presented must be addressed so that participants will be able to use it effectively.

Objectives will be written differently for each program so as to address the purpose of the program. The purpose may be to

(a) provide information or increase understanding, (b) improve physical skills, or (c) change awareness and attitudes.

If the purpose of the program deals with just the transmission of information, the objectives could include statements such as these:

Participants will be able to:

- Better understand new legislation
- Recognize the value of new approaches to management
- Increase their awareness of the implications of recent research

There is no emphasis on what participants will do with the information, but that is not the responsibility of the program.

An example of objectives developed where the purpose of the program is to improve skills could be:

The participants will be able to:

- Access the backup files of a computer software program
- Demonstrate proficiency in tying basic knots used in fire fighting
- Pass a test required by their association for renewed certification

Proficiency is the key, and the standards must be clear so that they can be objectively measured.

Objectives which address change in participants' attitudes tend to be the most difficult ones to measure because there is a combination of information provided and change suggested. In an example where the purpose of the program is to address attitudes, the objectives could include:

Participants will be able to:

- Demonstrate acceptance of cultural diversity in the workplace
- Work better with physically challenged coworkers
- Be more sensitive to the problems faced by newly hired workers

These objectives signify intent. Measuring the degree to which they are reached can be very difficult.

Whatever the objectives, they can be used to plan learning activities, to identify who will speak or make presentations, and to prepare these individuals so they can be effective in their presentations.

Implicit Objectives

Implicit objectives are the objectives participants will not see and are not in the marketing material. They can be shaped during all parts of the planning process, and those planning the program should discuss and agree upon them. They should be written into the program plan. There could be a variety of implicit objectives which address considerations not directly related to the educational dimensions of the program.

One objective could be building strong relationships among cosponsors. A second might be establishing a niche for a new program among a group not usually served. Another could be related to change and modest risk taking; this could include making active participant involvement a part of the program where lectures had been the norm. Implicit objectives may be broad institutional goals of a cosponsor.

There should be implicit objectives for every program, regardless of whether it is being run for the first time or has been in existence for 20 years. With these objectives, attention can be paid to ways to improve overall quality and the nature of the relationships that have contributed to the program's success.

LEARNING ACTIVITIES

How the objectives will be fulfilled depends upon the learning activities identified and developed. The material to be presented will help you determine which approaches are used. The subject matter may vary between concrete facts and abstract ideas, between theory and practice-based knowledge, and between complex and simple issues. Traditions and how participants expect to learn also play an important part in this determination. Cost is also a major determining factor.

Choosing Learning Activities

Attention to a number of factors will guide you in choosing and developing appropriate learning activities. Choosing the right activities can have a significant effect on the success of the program. You cannot isolate any one particular factor. We have provided ten factors that you should consider when choosing learning activities.

Characteristics of the Participants

Learner characteristics can be divided into group and individual characteristics. The participants will come as a group from a particular sector of your programming market, for example, community education, professional education, recreation, and adult basic education. Each sector of education may be better served by a particular approach to learning.

Second, each participant must be considered as an individual. Age, gender, ethnicity, level of prior education, knowledge of topic and level of skills, and physical or learning challenges faced by the participants must be factored into your choices. Earlier we discussed theories of adult learning. You should review this information as you consider how the characteristics of the participants influence the choice of learning activities.

Degree of Participant Involvement Needed to Satisfy Program Objectives

When the intent is to pass on information alone, participants can be passive listeners, for the most part, except when asking questions. In situations where performance is to be improved or attitudes changed, greater involvement will be necessary.

Pace of the Program and the Amount of Material to Be Provided

If information builds on a base of knowledge, obviously the pace can be faster or the load on participants heavier. When the area is completely new to participants, a slower pace, repetition of material, and a large number of examples will be important.

How Participants Expect to Learn

Participants may be most comfortable as passive learners taking notes from presentations by experts. Others may want an opportunity to discuss the material presented before asking questions. A third group may want a minimum amount of lecture and a maximum amount of time spent on practice or trial.

Tolerance for the New and Different

Some participants expect to be involved in some risk-taking at programs because they must use these new approaches in their work. Others may find new approaches threatening, especially those requiring involvement. Tolerance for the new and different today includes acceptance of technology, computers, and distance learning technology.

Mix of Learning Activities

The type of participant audience will determine how much is expected or to be avoided. The mix could include balancing heavy and demanding presentations with somewhat lighter ones. A second approach could include balancing information presented with opportunities for participants to discuss the implications of that information for practice.

Interaction Time for Participants

Time for participants to interact is not a learning activity in the strictest sense, but it is considered essential for many participants. For many, a principal reason for coming to a continuing education program is to meet informally with colleagues. At breaks, luncheons, or in unscheduled time they have an opportunity to discuss problems and share their approaches to solving them.

Time Needed to Absorb Material

If participants must demonstrate proficiency with the material, before they are tested you must include opportunities to practice what has been learned. You may need to schedule review sessions. If participants are to apply the information when they return to their jobs, time should be scheduled to determine how this will be done and expert support provided.

Program Location and Facilities

You must consider the fit between the learning activity and the learning situation. Ideal learning activities for a program may be restricted by the suitability of facilities or by the logistics of conducting those activities. Only one small room may be available for the program. It may be unsuitable for effective seating formats or larger groups. Appropriate technology may be unavailable. A location may be noisy because other events are going on simultaneously. An important factor to consider is the time of the day. For example, some methods are not suitable for afternoon sessions when participants may be beginning to tire. A slide presentation in a darkened room soon after lunch is a sure way of losing an audience.

Speakers' Preferred Methods of Presentation and Areas of Proficiency

The speakers and instructors in the program may have preferred ways of presenting their information. In addition, there may be particular methods in which they are more proficient than others. Those preferences and proficiencies must be determined and accommodated. They could be the exact opposite of the approach to learning that you want to use in the program.

You may have to guide the presenter in deciding on the approach most suitable considering all other factors.

Specific Learning Activities

As you review the list of specific learning activities, consider what each one might offer as a way for participants to obtain needed information, to build required skills, or to consider appropriate changes in behavior and attitude. You also should look at how blending activities together can produce the kind of mix that will be both attractive to potential participants and educationally sound.

The context in which the program is conducted will have a significant effect on the learning activity. There are a multitude of providers of continuing education, and each will have learning activities which are best suited to the content of their programs, their identified audience, and the objectives of their programs. This is not to suggest that you should always stay with a tried and tested formula. Be prepared to expose learners to new learning activities. However, learners may not be ready to "attend" to the learning. Consider phasing in new learning experiences over time.

Caffarella (1988) suggests that learning activities will be either individual learning, small group learning, or large group learning. The opportunities for participants to learn alone may be limited, but there should be many opportunities for small and large group learning. A program can include individual learning activities as well as learning in a variety of group sizes. For example, individual learning activities may be a prerequisite to participation in discussion groups, or discussion groups may be used to dissect the contents of a lecture. Again, the explicit objectives provide direction on what approach may be the most suitable. Learning activities include:

- Lecture
- Discussion
- Forum, panel, and symposium

- Simulation
- Workshop
- Print material and workbooks
- Communications technology
- Demonstrations and field trips

Galbraith (1990) provides a very descriptive outline of methods and techniques of adult learning. For further reading we suggest Apps (1991), Cranton (1989), Galbraith (1991), and Laird (1985). For further description of learning activities, see Appendix B.

Speakers and Other Forms of Expertise

As one of the introductory examples emphasized, major speakers can be a crucial ingredient. A person whose name is recognized can be a powerful attraction. Even the most sophisticated audiences will enjoy being mesmerized by an eloquent speaker. That is not to say you should not be wary of the "entertainer" who may be very appropriate in a situation requiring light relief in an otherwise demanding program, but who is not appreciated by an audience that demands expert knowledge in a forthright manner. An enthusiastic, well prepared presenter can overcome many of the negative aspects of a program that may result, for example, from inadequate facilities, or even an unresponsive audience. That presenter may be the saviour of your program.

Selecting the persons who will present content is an integral part of the successful development of the educational aspect of the program. In determining who should be invited to present, consider your objectives, planned learning activities, and the composition of your audience. Another source of influence on your decision will be who the participants expect to hear. Participants know the experts who are credible in their field and whose views are highly regarded. Most importantly, look for a presenter with the ability to carry the program in the most difficult of circumstances. Other criteria which you should consider include:

- Expertise in and enthusiasm for content
- Appreciation and understanding of adults as learners
- Enjoyment when working with adults
- Effective platform skills
- Appropriate sense of humor
- Willingness to be creative and innovative
- Ability to adjust presentation to accommodate learners
- Organization and preparedness.

Expert program planners have developed systems for finding these individuals and making sure they can do the job, including:

- Ways to check on speakers' performances at similar programs
- Contacts with colleagues to determine if speakers presented any difficulties, made unusual or unrealistic demands, or were unreliable
- Research to ensure the speaker does not have publicly expressed views which may conflict with the cosponsors or participants
- Conversations with the speakers to ensure that they are genuinely interested in making a presentation and that they have time to adequately prepare for the event
- Checks with cosponsors and others key to the program's success to determine the speaker's contribution to the event
- A final review of all selected speakers to ensure an appropriate balance and comprehensiveness to meet participant expectations.

Once these steps have been taken, you should make sure that all those who will speak, present, appear on a panel, or make some contribution are provided with adequate information including:

- A copy of the brochure and detail on the entire program
- Details of the material they must prepare in advance and due dates
- Guidelines for making travel arrangements

- Facilities and instructional resources available and instructions for ordering necessary equipment and room setup requirements
- Forms to be completed to receive any compensation due

All of these items are routinely provided to speakers and others who contribute to a program. Less likely to be provided are:

- Details on participants and their level of familiarity with the topic
- The role the speakers' presentation plays in the program
- The topics that should be covered in the presentation
- Details of other speakers and their topics
- A list of cosponsors and their role in the program
- Any particular issues the speaker should approach with caution
- Conventions to be observed when speaking with this group.

Too often expertise and familiarity with the audience are taken for granted. There may be awe of an expert that prevents informing the presenter about what is expected. The results can be less than desired.

Today it is very important to make sure all arrangements are clear and complete. Formal contracts are used in some situations; a detailed letter may suffice at other times. In either case, both the presenter and a program representative should sign these documents. Finally, do not forget to reconfirm with the speakers and presenters a day or two prior to the event. This can be done in a way that reaffirms to them your enthusiasm for their participation in the program, while reassuring yourself that another program detail is in hand.

CLIMATE AND SETTING

Climate and setting are the final two elements that should be considered here and often are not given sufficient attention. They are the two closely-tied factors that build an environment comfortable to participants. They will add to the appeal of the program. Where a program is held is only one portion of this important combination. Climate and setting interplay with what we know as group dynamics. Group dynamics go further than the physical to include interpersonal relationships and self-knowledge.

Dimensions of Climate and Setting

Hiemstra (1991) suggests that learning environments are complex and influenced by a number of variables. Consider setting in a broad sense and ask the following questions:

- Does the setting contribute to or enhance the status of the program?
- Is the setting conducive to the absorption of learning?
- Is the setting receptive to appropriate methods of learning?

Knox (1990) emphasizes that a challenging setting is "neither boring nor threatening, (and) promotes worthwhile educational achievement" (p. 132).

Provisions must be made to make individuals feel comfortable and for people to meet and become acquainted. Participants should be made to feel welcome at the same time they learn about the specifics of the program. You can begin to establish the climate for the program through advance publicity. Participants will be more comfortable knowing these details up front. Identification of cosponsors, planners, and other participants and encouraging participants to ask questions or provide suggestions for improving the program or amenities help create a positive climate. There are four aspects to setting and climate that you should consider as you determine appropriate learning activities.

Physical Environment

The physical environment affects learning. Consider not only the room size and structure, but access, lighting, temperature, color, the general aesthetic of the room, and proximity of amenities.

Psychological Climate

There must be a climate of mutual respect of individual experiences and diversity and a warm, friendly, and supportive environment. Encourage collaboration rather than competition, and emphasize learning rather than teaching. In this way you break down negative feelings toward the authority which participants may feel the presenter holds.

Social Environment

The opening moments of a program or learning activity will have the greatest impact on the participants. Create a sense of community, sharing, and hospitality.

Cultural and Political Setting

Cosponsors will impact the environment simply by their involvement. All organizations have a culture and operate within a political structure. We define the culture of the organization as the way it does things, the way it treats its people. It goes beyond such issues as the recognition of diversity.

LEGAL CONSIDERATIONS

In planning and delivering programs, you should be aware of the legal issues which may impact the provision of the program. Areas to consider include for example, copyright law as it pertains to limits on what materials can be duplicated for participant use. This could also include the use of copyright broadcast materials such as video taped television programs, even the use of copyright works of art in promotional material.

Legal issues go beyond copyright. Depending on the context and the cosponsors of programs, you may need to consider the law relating to contracts and negligence. In most programs, contracts will exist between the program planner, cosponsors, and the providers of services, facilities, even those presenting material in the program. These contracts provide the legal basis for securing those facilities and services and spell out in detail the rights and obligations of both parties including recourse where one of the parties fails to deliver its part of the bargain. The laws of contract apply here as they do in any business transaction. You should be aware of what you are committing yourself and others to when signing a contract.

The issue of negligence is far more complicated and very little has been written on negligence as it applies to providers of continuing education. Most cases come from the school setting and to a lesser extent from the higher education setting, where it is the institution which is involved in litigation. Schroeder (1992) has written about legal liability and the Cooperative Extension Service as a provider of continuing education. He provides a good summary of the law relating to negligence as well as how it may affect a service organization. Hobbs (1982) and Cote and McAfee (1987) address similar issues as they apply to institutions of higher education including continuing higher education.

In this book we cannot possibly address all the issues that may arise out of negligence. There are two issues we can raise here. One is that you have a duty to provide a safe environment for participants and, in a program which involves hands-on participation, proper supervision and instruction must be provided to reduce your liability in cases of injury. Another issue is being able to deliver on any express warranties which you may include in publicity material for a course. For example, if you state that completion of the program will lead to certification or that it will satisfy certain licensing criteria, then it must do so or you may be liable.

There are other legal issues which arise in all business transactions, such as laws relating to employment, including sexual harassment, affirmative action, and Americans with disabilities provisions. Taxation is another area of the law which may have an effect on program planning. This could include sales tax on sales of program booklets, materials and souvenirs, and income taxes as they relate to employees. Other provisions relate to workers' compensation and insurance protection. Knowledge of the consequences of negligent acts and violation of statutory provisions can reduce the potential for litigation. Question the legal implications of your actions and inform those who work with you in the planning process of their responsibilities, and in all cases of doubt seek legal counsel.

CONTINUOUS EVALUATION

Ideally, the evaluation process begins when the basic concept is completed. Hastily prepared evaluations administered at the conclusion of a program often are of very little worth. More than just the actual program can be evaluated. The effectiveness of the development and planning process, the strength of working relationships among cosponsors, the ease of completing necessary tasks, and participant services are just a few of the areas that you can assess. By developing a commitment to evaluation from the start, you can continually gather valuable information. Changes can be made in how the program is to be planned and operated. In some cases, an early and intelligent decision to cancel the program could be made.

Right from the start, a basic question has to be answered: What role does evaluation play in this program? In some situations, the answer will indicate that little is expected to be learned from evaluation. The program may be so well established and continually successful that planners feel they don't need the reactions and advice that evaluations can provide. That is one perspective to avoid.

At the other extreme, planners may want to do an exhaustive evaluation, asking participants to judge each and every aspect of the program in tedious detail. Then, participants may tire of responding, and the value of reactions and advice is lost.

A balanced approach is most desirable. The evaluation should assess the overall value of the program to the participants, assess whether specific dimensions of the program are appropriate, and provide useful information for making informed decisions. Build on your existing understanding of the program to develop your evaluation (Knox, 1990).

Evaluations can be generalized as formative or summative (Kowalski, 1988). Formative evaluations of the process and effectiveness of the program aid in improving the current program or in planning future programs. Summative evaluation is an appraisal of the success or worth of the program. This type of evaluation is used to assess program impact on the participants or to argue for continued support from sponsors.

In developing a program evaluation ask yourself:

- What will be evaluated?
- What will the responses tell me about the program's effectiveness?
- Who will conduct and monitor the evaluation?
- How will the results be used?

To answer the first question, consider aspects of the program in broad terms rather than being explicit about every detail. Ask for further explanation only if appropriate. Short carefully developed evaluations may produce information of greater value than a long, poorly constructed form.

In most programs provide participants an opportunity to react to:

1. The topic covered

2. The instructors or presenters

3. Any materials provided

4. The physical arrangements including location

5. The advance registration and on-site registration procedures

6. Aspects of the program that do not fit into the above categories

In Figure 4.1 and Figure 4.2 you will find a short evaluation to which participants can respond in less than three minutes. The

PROGRAM EVALUATION
REVENUE ENHANCEMENT WORKSHOP SERIES
June 20, 1994

Please complete this evaluation and give to the program host as you leave.

1. Please evaluate these aspects of the program using a five-point scale.

	Poor		Fair		Good
a. Preprogram information	1	2	3	4	5
b. Registration procedures	1	2	3	4	5

2. Please evaluate the program content using a five-point scale.

	Poor		Fair		Good
a. Overview by John Jones	1	2	3	4	5
b. Presentation by Carol Smith	1	2	3	4	5
c. Presentation by Clyde Brown	1	2	3	4	5
d. Materials provided	1	2	3	4	5
e. Opportunities for discussion	1	2	3	4	5

3. Please describe what you gained most from this workshop.

_____

_____

4. In what ways could future workshops be improved? Please explain.

_____

_____

Thank you. Your suggestions are appreciated.

Figure 4.1   Sample program evaluation

EVALUATION
COMMUNITY COLLABORATION SEMINAR
March 25, 1994

Please assist us with responses to the following questions and return your completed evaluation to the seminar director before you leave. Please circle your response. Your comments are appreciated. Thank you.

	Agree				Disagree
1. The collaboration model was clearly presented and explained.	1	2	3	4	5
2. Discussion of the pilot programs helped me understand the approach.	1	2	3	4	5
3. There was adequate time for questions and discussion.	1	2	3	4	5
4. The facilities were appropriate.	1	2	3	4	5
5. The location was convenient.	1	2	3	4	5

6. In what ways could the program be
   improved? Please give your suggestions below.

_____

_____

_____

_____

7. What other topics related to school-community collaboration should be addressed in future seminars? Please list suggestions below.

_____

_____

_____

_____

Figure 4.2   Sample program evaluation

number of forms completed is likely to be higher than for a longer evaluation form.

For the majority of programs where simplified forms are used, program personnel can develop the evaluation instrument, implement and monitor the evaluation, tally the results, and prepare a report. The cost in time and money of developing, monitoring, and reporting the results of an evaluation further reinforces our point of keeping it succinct. In some cases, cosponsors may have certain evaluation requirements. An outsider, whose work will be more objective, might do the evaluation. The "outsider" should be involved in the planning process from the beginning.

The evaluation results will be used by a number of groups including the planning committee, cosponsors, and financial supporters. Participants who know that evaluation results are used in planning are more apt to cooperate. Do not evaluate a program if the results will not be used.

Qualitative information can be a useful addition to quantitative data gathered from completed evaluation forms. Comments can be gathered from participants, speakers, and other instructors. The planning committee itself can be asked to evaluate the planning process, as well as the program. When combined with the quantitative information, qualitative responses allow a more complete picture of the program to emerge.

One aspect of summative evaluation cannot always be done immediately following the program; namely, the impact of the program on the participants and their subsequent performance, and the effect that participants then have on the community, business, or organization where they work. These effects may not be felt for some time. If appropriate, you need to design your evaluation to accommodate longer term impact. Sponsors may also assume responsibility for the longer-term evaluation.

As the program planner, your own subjective evaluation is very important. Working closely with the program, you should have a good idea of its strengths and weaknesses. Be sure to make notes as you proceed with the planning. However, bear in mind that being so close to the program can blind you to some truths that you would prefer not to see and can compromise your objectivity. Conversely, recognizing your successes may be as difficult as being self-critical.

Much has been written on evaluation models, methods, and the forms evaluation may take. Further reading includes Beatty, Benefield & Linhart, 1991; Brookfield, 1986; Deshler, 1984; Guba & Lincoln, 1981; Houle, 1972; and Steele, 1990. Listed here are several methods of gathering data that may be beneficial in planning an evaluation:

- Rating scales and checklists
- Questionnaires
- Pre- and post-tests
- Observation
- Group discussion
- Personal interview
- Focus groups
- Work samples

The selection of the evaluation method or methods will be determined by the focus of the evaluation. The focus may vary for the individual components or activities of the program. The evaluation may also be focused for the different people involved in the planning process, whether they be the organizing committee, cosponsors, or participants, or depending on who has requested the evaluation. Finally, it may be appropriate to follow up on the evaluation. You may wish to construct your evaluation to allow respondents to provide their name so that you can contact them at a later date to have them elaborate on their responses or to invite them to participate in planning the next program. Also, if you have forwarded a copy of the evaluation report to cosponsors and participants, you may solicit their reaction to the report.

SUMMARY

As you start to plan the content of the continuing education program, you need to begin with a good understanding of how adults learn. It is difficult to generalize for each program, but by establishing who your potential audience will be, those basic theories can be a very useful guide in setting objectives and the associated learning activities. Selecting speakers who relate well to adult learners will enhance the learning activities.

We have stressed that establishing an appropriate environment for learning through attention to climate and setting and group dynamics might be the most crucial planning element. Remember, it is the learner who is at the heart of the program planning process. Create a positive image from the very beginning through publicity for the program.

Two final elements of planning which we have addressed are attention to the legal issues which are forever present in all contractual situations and the need for continuous evaluation of the program and planning process. Evaluation is the basis for improvement of existing programs and for developing successful new programs.

CHAPTER 5

Managing Budgets and Marketing

At first glance, the two categories may seem ill-matched and unlikely to be addressed in the same chapter. The joining, however, was done with a purpose: to underline just how much attention must be paid to costs that can easily escalate to the detriment of a program. One cost that could do so very rapidly is marketing.

A program that is new and attempting to enter an already crowded market will have high marketing expenses. Add the cost of a major speaker needed to attract participants, and very quickly you have a high fixed cost component. This may require a high registration fee to recoup these expenses.

For an already established program, the marketing costs are far less. Where the first program starts with a distinct disadvantage, cost control is far more likely with the second program. The marketing that is done retains the program's audience by stressing its continuing quality.

In years to come as competition remains strong, marketing a program will continue to be a major concern and the costs associated with this task a major part of many budgets. As budgets are developed, effective program planners continue to ask if there is enough willingness to spend the money necessary to secure sufficient registrations.

A marketing plan with identifiable limits is necessary. Constantly supplementing basic marketing with haphazard additional efforts leads to budget disaster. For programs with a history, past efforts and their results provide guidance on how much should be done. Newer programs require comparison with similar programs to assess what mix of brochures, adver-

tisements, and other notices is likely to produce the desired results.

The link between the two areas will be further explored
in this chapter. We will consider the development of a working
budget as a part of the program and the calculation of fixed and
variable expenses. Instituting cost control measures and shaping registration fees will be addressed as we look toward establishing realistic financial goals. In the second part of the
chapter we will discuss the significance of marketing in the
planning process. We will offer some advice on marketing approaches and the necessary ingredients in effective marketing
material.

HOW TO DEVELOP A BUDGET

Budgeting is both a planning process and a communication
process (Matkin, 1985). The document should communicate to
others the educational program in financial terms. A working
budget is just what the name indicates, a document that you
work on as the program evolves and one that works for you. In
Chapter Four, you read comments that indicated the educational
portion of the program shouldn't get in the way of meals and social activities. Those whose concerns may be financial could say
that the educational portion of the program shouldn't get in the
way of a sound budget.

Effective budget planners (Bennet & LeGrand, 1990; Caffarella, 1988; Simerly, 1993) make the same point. The program
should drive the budget, not the contrary. With a clear concept
for the program, and sound objectives, you can identify what it
will cost to make the program a reality.

Later in this chapter fixed and variable costs will be explained in some detail. As those costs are identified, you and others involved in planning can determine if the budget figures for
both expenditures and income are accurate and realistic. Accuracy is easy enough to achieve, if you have sound information
and a good calculator.

The realistic part is another matter. Serious thought and
good judgment are needed to calculate certain expenditures

such as how much to spend on marketing a program or what compensation to offer a speaker. A realistic budget is conservative when projecting income and pessimistic when identifying costs. Pessimism involves expecting items to cost more and unplanned expenses to occur. When you have identified likely costs and potential income, you can be realistic and determine if the program makes sense, from a financial perceptive.

Bennett and LeGrand (1990), among others, have spent many years developing budgets for programs. As part of the guidance they provide, these skilled scholar-practitioners stress accuracy. Accuracy requires that every possible cost no matter how small, is identified, and a category of miscellaneous expenses included for unanticipated and forgotten items.

As all costs are identified, realism enters in two other ways. First, you and other planners can ask questions about "need." Is this activity really needed? Can we afford to have this person speak? Is it really necessary to have a lunch just as people are leaving? Will participants really use all the material we plan to duplicate?

The second dimension of reality addresses the potential participants and how much they will be willing to pay to attend the program. Participants recognize that to enjoy an educational experience, they may have to pay a substantial fee. However, they do have limits which are based, in part, on what they have paid in the past and what they believe they will get for their money. What participants expect to pay figures into their registration decision. This could be a substantial or limited amount. In marketing it is called a "price point," beyond which customers will not go.

Potential participants also think about what other costs they will have to absorb to attend a program. Transportation to the program site, lost income, and incidental expenses are three costs likely to be considered. Although not figured into your program budget, you must be aware of them, because if these costs are substantial participants may decide not to attend the program regardless of the registration fee.

There are four phases in the budget development and management process, parallel to the process of shaping other aspects of the program. "Shaping" is an important word. Thanks to spreadsheet technology, changes can be made easily. A great deal of the truly artistic shaping of a budget, of course, takes place during the early stages of program planning. Since enough of the unexpected will occur as a program is being marketed or even while operating, shaping will be needed at these stages, too.

At an early stage, the planners may have an idea for a new program and want to see if the "numbers will work" when costs are matched with projected numbers and the willingness of potential participants to pay a registration fee. Using spreadsheets, different combinations of expenses and income can be developed and examined. Different registration fees can be calculated using a number of participant levels. These numbers are powerful, because of the "what if . . ." scenarios they create. Figure 5.1 is a budget showing the budget breakdown for three levels of participation and a registration fee based on the low estimate of attendance.

Budgets are built and shaped. Effective planners ask those who may be the content specialists or representatives of the participants a number of questions that help with the building and shaping process. Those questions include but are not limited to the following:

1. How many participants have attended past continuing education programs? Can you expect the same number, more or less? Why?

2. What have participants been willing to pay to attend past programs?

3. Who must speak or present at the program and how much will they have to be paid? How much will it cost to get them to the program?

4. How much marketing will have to be done and in what form? Will mailing lists have to be purchased? Will advertising have to purchased?

5. How much written and other materials will participants receive?

6. How long will the program last? How many meals and other food service and social events will be held?

7. Where will the program be held and what will it cost?

8. Are any subsidies from sponsors or grants available to underwrite some of the costs of the program?

Through these and other questions, all activities that cost money can be determined. You can then start discussing a fee range that participants would be willing to meet and that fits with the type and amount of expenses anticipated. If the fee range which would cover expenses seems reasonable, a more detailed budget can be developed.

When it appears that the concept and the numbers work and a decision to operate the program has been made, a second type of budget is developed with tentative costs identified. It is the focal point for discussion and manipulation. Through discussion, planners and cosponsors determine what amount of money has to be allocated to which fixed categories. Manipulation begins and continues as decisions are made to reduce or add amounts to both fixed and variable categories.

Review takes place constantly, daily in some situations, as both expenses and income are checked. Monitoring is especially valuable so that intelligent spot decisions can be made. These include: printing extra brochures for an additional marketing effort; adding a speaker; deleting a meal; limiting how much material will be duplicated for participants. With a budget whose figures can be manipulated, a planner can look at the consequences of any decision made. Review continues until the program is completed. Remember that you may find the number of registrations is far lower than expected and you may have to cancel a program and find a way to absorb marketing and other costs. This is a risk to consider.

The wrap up occurs after the program is over, all income has been received, and all bills paid. Then a final statement can be prepared showing what really happened. Did the program make or lose money? How much was made or lost? What can be learned from this experience? These are questions you can answer with what amounts to a profit and loss statement.

Figure 5.1 Sample budget form

Sample Budget Form

Submitted by: John Black   **Preparation date:**
Program title: Update on APA
Date(s): 8/16/94
Location(s): Champaign Regency

	Estimated	Actual
Evaluations		
Duplication	35	—
Analysis	—	—
On-site		
Facilities rental	200	—
Physical plant	—	—
A-V equipment	150	—
Equipment rental	200	—
Entertainment	—	—
Photography	—	—
General administrative expenses		
Administrative fee	1000	—
Administrative travel	100	—
General duplicating	75	—
Telephone/FAX	50	—
Mailing	75	—
Other	—	—
Total fixed costs	7635	—
Estimated attendance	75	—
Fixed fee per person	101.80	—
(Total ÷ estimated attendance)		

Per Person Registration Fee Summary

Fixed fee per person: 101.80   Variable fee per person: 39.93
Final registration fee: 150.00

Total Budget Breakdown

	Estimated Attendance			
	Low	Medium	High	Actual
	75	100	125	
A. Total fixed costs	7635	7635	7635	—
B. Variable fee × number of participants	2995	3993	4991	—
C. Total program costs	10630	11628	12626	—
D. Other contributions				—
E. Balance	10630	11628	12626	—
F. Balance ÷ estimated attendance	142	117	101	—
G. ___ % cushion	5	5	5	—

H. Registration fee × number of participants	11250	15000	18750	—
I. Total income (D + H)	11250	15000	18750	—
J. Profit (loss) (I − C)	620	3372	6124	—

Worksheet

Faculty member	Travel	Honorarium	Other	Total	Date paid
G. Jones	650	750	—	—	—
L. Walker	650	500	—	—	—
A. Burke	500	650	—	—	—
Total faculty expenses				3700	—

Fixed Costs

	Estimated	Actual
Total faculty expenses	3700	—
Planning committee		
Travel		—
Meals		—
Other		—
Promotion		
Brochure graphic design	100	—
Typesetting	150	—
Brochure printing	700	—
Brochure mailing	900	—
Other advertising	200	—

Variable Costs Per Person

	Estimated	Actual
Participant confirmation	3	—
Participant handouts		—
Duplicating	7	—
Notebook		—
Paper and pencils	2	—
Proceedings		—
Meals		—
Breakfast		—
Lunch	14	—
Dinner		—
Banquet		—
Break(s) 2 @ $3.50	7	—
Reception		—
Tax and gratuity 21%	6.93	—
Credit card percentage (%)		—
Total per person available	39.93	—

Approvals

Where Does the Income Come From?

Income is the money that will pay the bills. As a part of the budgeting process you must determine where that income will come from. The financial goal of the program is an initial consideration which will affect the level of income. This will have been decided when developing the basic concept. Obviously we would like to return a profit on all our endeavors, and at worst break even.

There may be a reason, however, to consider accepting something less than break-even. It may be to use the program as a promotional exercise to introduce a new topic into a community or to introduce the concept of continuing education to a community. It may be to assess the viability of future programs. That is not to say you proceed with the foolish attitude of accepting a loss of any size. You still must work within a budget. Income can come from a number of sources.

Registration Fees

In most programs participants will be required to pay a fee to attend the program. The fee is calculated at a break-even point to cover all expenses. Shaping registration fees is covered in detail later in the chapter.

Cosponsors

Various sponsors may contribute financial or other resources to a program. This may be in return for publicity or it may be as the result of the sponsor's commitment to continuing education in a particular area or a commitment to community development and other social issues. The contribution may be in kind, that is goods and services.

Grants and Subsidies

Various government and private agencies and foundations may contribute funds to support programming. These funds may be offered as part of a cosponsorship arrangement, but they may also be obtained through writing grant proposals. Soliciting financial contributions is another way.

Product Sales

As a part of the program, you may sell items such as mementos of the program, or printed materials or proceedings (although these are generally factored into the registration fee). Income from product sales might not be used in the program budget but kept as a separate account. However, any surplus from these sales can be used to subsidize the program or to provide a buffer against unforeseen expenses.

In-kind Contributions and Volunteer Time

No funds are received for in-kind contributions and for volunteer time, and they are not shown on the budget in dollar terms. However, it is important to recognize the effect that these have on the budget. These contributions of materials, services, and time reduce the expenses for the program and are reflected in the registration fee and the bottom line finances. Recording this information is important for planning future programs. It serves to illustrate to cosponsors just how expensive it would be to conduct a program without in-kind contributions and volunteer assistance. It also provides a record of who to express appreciation to at the conclusion of the program.

What Are Fixed and Variable Costs?

Over the years effective program planners have been able to reduce the budget process to a few simple but effective management concepts. The two most important are carefully dividing each budget into clear fixed and variable costs. The fixed group includes those costs that a program will incur, regardless of the number of participants; in that category are some of the large expense items such as fees for speakers and all of the costs associated with marketing, from the charges for graphic work to purchasing mailing lists.

One potentially controversial fixed cost is the amount charged for those involved in planning a program or handling its administrative arrangements. In some postsecondary educational institutions and professional associations, those who plan programs earn all or a part of their salary from program income. Overhead costs also are covered through this fee.

Bennett and LeGrand (1990) suggest two ways of calculating the administrative fee. One is to charge an amount for each hour of instruction provided in the program. A second is to calculate total program costs and then take a percentage of that total. There are other methods, and each planner who must set an administrative fee should think very carefully about what is being provided, what those services actually cost, and what adjustments have to be made so that the fee is compatible with the rest of the program's budget.

One last budget item is the miscellaneous category. The percentage of total costs used to determine that amount varies from a low of three percent up to 15 percent. A sense of what unplanned costs could arise will guide the calculation of this charge. Past experience with similar programs also helps.

As the name suggests, variable costs are driven by the number of people attending the program. Anything provided to a participant that he or she alone receives is a variable cost. The cost of food, charges for duplicating material, books provided, and lodging expenses fall into this category. The total variable cost increases as the number of registrations increase.

Each meal, coffee break, piece of paper, souvenir and name tag was purchased and must be paid for. There have been programs where registrations substantially exceeded expectations yet still lost money because the per item variable costs were not accurate and not recoverable.

Those who champion a program may feel that there is a ready audience for it. Planners with experience who know what really happens will be more conservative and likely to suggest that fewer will attend.

A goal is to reach the lowest possible break-even number of participants. That means that costs have to be held down or some other subsidies found to provide a financial cushion. As mentioned earlier in this book, some programs maintain a loyal following from having such a strong history of being valuable experiences that high numbers can be legitimately projected. Still, forces beyond the control of the planners can lower the registration total. In all cases, conservatism is advised; plan for higher expenses and lower income. Dealing with an unantici-pated surplus is a lot more fun than trying to determine how to cover a deficit.

What Cost Control Measures Are Possible?

Regardless of a program's stability, cost control is always an important management activity. In some situations, there may be funds to add to the overall attractiveness of the program. Even then, experienced planners show prudence, lest the addition of a fancy dinner or social event be interpreted as an extravagant use of participants' registration fees.

In most situations, however, you and others involved in planning this program will want to identify ways to reduce the size of the budget. For most of the categories on the fixed cost side, some tightening is possible without harming the program's overall intent. You could, for example, determine if some speak-ers will accept a smaller fee. An external sponsor may be willing to pay part of a speaker's fee. Some programs offer honorariums that have a low base fee which increases with the number of reg-istrations.

Marketing expenses could be controlled. An attractive but less costly brochure could be prepared; one color rather than sev-eral is an option to consider. The size of the mailing list could be limited.

Look for a location for the program that will cost less yet still offer very attractive facilities. Consider the location not only in terms of its base cost, but additional expenses including those incurred due to travel distance, cost to bring in additional equip-ment, transportation of computing and other equipment to set up a "site" office. Be innovative in choosing the formats and menus for meals and breaks in the proceedings. The program could start later in the morning and end earlier in the day to cut down on the number of meal functions. Fewer materials could be duplicated, with a limit set on how much each speaker or panelist should submit to be copied and distributed.

You can see there are numerous options to consider. We have offered only a few here. As you review budget categories, ask questions about what can be cut without doing damage to the program. If you understand the participants and their expectations, those cuts will be accepted and even applauded.

How Can Registration Fees Be Shaped?

As Simerly (1993) has emphasized, with the agreement of many of his colleagues, a major goal should be to reach the budget break-even point (where income and expenses match) with the lowest number of registrants. Realism shaped by bitter experience is one reason why this approach has been taken more and more by program planners.

Low registration fees and unrealistically high projections of the number who will attend are a formula for disaster. Higher registration fees based on a conservative projection of numbers is sound planning. Past experience will be some guide, but you want to avoid the trap of thinking that an equal or larger number will attend the next program. Cut estimates for repeat programs by a least 30 percent; for first time programs, cutting original projections back by 60 to 70% is realistic conservatism.

You may want to consider different ways to charge for registration, beyond a single one. Treat these possibilities with great care and check your figures very carefully before offering them. You could be hurting yourself with them. These alternative fee schedules include:

- Discount for early registration. Experienced planners use the figure established as the actual cost for registration and then add 10 to 15% as the fee for registrations after the early-bird date.
- Discounts for two or more participants from the same organization. Careful monitoring is important. If this is a small program, these discounts could have a substantial impact on the registration income.

- A base fee and separate registration fees for individual events. This menu of events is attractive and is common at large national meetings. Extra work is generated in handling the individual registrations.

While shaping the registration fee, you must set a policy to cover cancellations and no-shows who have prepaid. A certain percentage should be retained to cover administrative costs and variable expenses that cannot be recovered. Ensure that the cancellation policy is noted in the registration materials. A good business decision is to refund part of the fee, if possible, as a way of preserving patronage for future programs.

How to Set Realistic Financial Goals

Throughout the entire process of budget development, planners and all those included in decision-making should weigh what the financial goals of the program are. Ideally, all programs have enough participants and have been planned with such excellence that income exceeds expenses. But that is not a reality in many situations nor should it always be a goal.

Continuing education programs are planned and operated for various reasons. One, for example, could be to determine if there is an audience for a particular topic. Then some risks will have to be taken, including the possibility of losing money. In another situation, a program may be for an audience with limited financial means; then the goal would be to come as close to breaking even as possible.

In the business world, manufacturers take risks all of the time when they introduce new products. They know that only a small percentage of those that reach a market will survive. But risk they must to survive and to continue to expand their customer base.

Today, the same is true in continuing education of all types. Trial and retrial eventually lead to the identification of programs with a solid market. In the process, some money is lost, but it could be regained and then some in years to come.

Effective Budget Management

In summary, consider the following additional points as a guide to effective budget management

- Account for all activities which will incur expenses.
- Consider a fee range that is appropriate for the intended audience.
- Look at the ancillary costs of choosing a particular location.
- Determine the costs of administering the program on site.
- Institute a system of authority for "out-of-pocket" expenses prior to and during the program.
- Choose items that add distinctiveness to the program such as stationery and mementos which fit the audience and the budget.
- Consider small details such as the use of china rather than paper tableware to add distinctiveness while remaining within budget.
- Maintain control over the marketing plan.
- Control costs on publishing the proceedings of the program and decide whether to include it in the registration fee or to sell it separately to participants and through other sources.
- Plan meal functions, underestimate numbers, and add more later.
- Be clear on the number of complementary registrations and what each complementary is entitled to.
- Include expenses associated with managing volunteers.
- Monitor, monitor, monitor—recognize when you have overrun on a particular item, institute control measures, and try to balance out by cutting back on some other expenses.

WHY IS MARKETING SO SIGNIFICANT TODAY?

Marketing is the process of bringing together the supplier of a product and the potential consumer of that product. The consumers must decide to forgo some of their resources such as time, money, and leisure in exchange for some product that will improve their quality of life. There is a communication of information between the supplier and the consumer, and it is the quality of that communication which will determine the success of the marketing strategy. The communication must create awareness, provide information, and stimulate the potential consumer's interest in the product.

Marketing involves four interrelated factors: (a) the identification of a product, (b) the establishment of a price for the product which will be acceptable in the market, (c) the identification of the group to whom you will promote the product, and (d) the selection of the most effective combination of methods of promotion. Attention to each of these factors will form the basis of your marketing plan. Simerly (1989) suggests that marketing is not so much an activity as a process that is integral to the goals and objectives of your program planning organization. Promotional activities may sell the program but the program itself, the planning of that program, and the planning organization will be equally if not more important in the marketing.

Consumer decision making has been studied extensively, and that body of research is useful in developing a marketing plan for your program. The literature on continuing education is filled with normative and research based material on the importance of effective marketing. The authors believe that the *Handbook of Marketing for Continuing Education* (Simerly & Associates, 1989) is the most comprehensive and practice-based guide to effective marketing in continuing education, and it is recommended as a reference. In this section, a few of the key thoughts from some of the other literature will be summarized to establish a base for the suggested approach to controlling marketing costs that will be addressed in the rest of this chapter.

Yellen and Hussey (1990) stress just how competitive continuing education has become and remind planners that potential registrants will see a lot of marketing material. They emphasize how important it is to clearly articulate program benefits and "the image of the program" in whatever information and literature is provided. The obvious benefits of participation should be clear. These include job advancement and developing new personal skills. The not so obvious ones include improved self-esteem, meeting new friends, and more productive use of leisure time. Highlight the fun and rewards of participation.

Griffith (1989) and Smith and Offerman (1989) support this contention. Griffith adds the idea of a persuasive message that spells out what a participant will derive from registration. Further, he states the value of identifying what background and experience a participant should have to properly benefit from a program.

The importance of communicating enthusiasm in the marketing material is emphasized by Bennett and LeGrand (1990). They believe this enthusiasm is especially important when participants are required to attend a program by their employers or when attendance is mandated by a professional organization. Participants may approach it with levels of dread. Providing sufficient information for an informed choice is another component these authors urge planners to consider. Your program will be competing for the time and resources of potential participants with other programs, day-to-day activities, work, and family commitments. Keep these competing factors in mind when planning your marketing.

It is essential that all information in the marketing materials be accurate. We have addressed the legal issues of making false claims in advertising material in Chapter 4. Legal considerations aside, false or misleading advertising can seriously damage the program image. For example, if a prominent speaker such as a member of Congress has been invited to speak but is yet to confirm, indicate that fact in the material.

Dahl's (1993) contribution addresses the presentation dimension of the marketing material. She urges skill in writing marketing copy and a great deal of attention to the visual appeal. Quoting others with backgrounds in marketing for nonprofit organizations, Dahl ties graphic design and layout to the creation of a program image that attracts participants. Remember that with advertising, you control the message that goes out to the potential participant. Both words and image are a part of that message.

Gathering data on how participants learned about a program is an important aspect of an effective marketing plan. Identify how participants learned about a program and track their participation in programs to evaluate the return on your marketing investment.

Reflecting on trends in marketing adult and continuing education, Coates and Dobmeyer (1990) point out how much more of a role simplicity plays in brochure design today. Attractiveness and readability are primary concerns. Potential registrants must be able to read the information quickly and easily, without wondering what certain words mean. Less copy is a trend they have identified as part of an effort to make brochures, still the marketing mainstay, more capable of attracting the scant attention readers will give to them. Kreitlow (1990) adds a note of caution about the look of contemporary marketing material. He is concerned about the amount of "glitz and glitter" that now appears in marketing material.

Falk (1986) and Knox (1991) recognize the value of offering high quality programs as perhaps the best marketing tool. Knox says that "a powerful influence on a participant's decision to participate is word of mouth comments by satisfied participants' (p. 234). Both solicited and unsolicited comments on the quality of a program spread by word of mouth can be an inexpensive way of attracting new participants in the same way that quality programs will encourage repeat participants. But the programs must be of high quality and meet the needs of the intended audience. Don't forget that word of mouth can relate reports of poor quality programs too!

How Much and What Kind
of Marketing Should Be Done

As mentioned earlier and shown through the budget examples, marketing can be the single highest fixed cost for many programs. In fact, the drive to secure participants can produce a vicious circle of more money directed toward marketing to get more participants to pay for the cost of marketing. Today and in years to come, planners will have to ask themselves how much marketing will be necessary to secure the break-even number of participants, and do we have the money and the will for that sort of campaign?

Experience and program strength can reduce the amount of marketing required. Consider four types of programs and the impact of their status on the amount of marketing that has to be done.

- A very secure program offered successfully for more than five years with a steady or increasing number of participants may require a minimum amount of marketing to a narrowly identified audience.
- A second program has been offered for five years but attendance varied from year to year and thus the market is not yet secure. An extensive effort to reach past participants and others must be made.
- The third type of program has been offered once or twice, with some success but not enough to do any less than a full scale marketing effort utilizing a number of approaches.
- A final program will be offered for the first time; planners think they know who might attend but have to explore as many possibilities as their budget will allow.

Program history and status have a definite impact on the amount of marketing to be done, but other factors have to be considered too. First is the type of information that participants have indicated they expect or are used to receiving. Some groups need only what amounts to a handout announcement to make the decision to attend a program and would be insulted by a fancy brochure. "Spend the money on the program or lower the registration fee," they will say.

Cosponsors may want to have a say in what is presented; after all, their organization's name appears on the cover and they don't want to be surprised and embarrassed. A great deal of time can be spent getting agreement on what the cover will contain in the way of information, advertising and graphics, or the color of paper to be used.

A second consideration is the necessary complexity of the brochure. Elements that should be included to create an effective brochure include:

1. A well-conceived and written message

2. A clear title

3. Identification of cosponsors

4. Date(s), times and location of the event

5. The intended audience for the program

6. Program objectives and topics to be covered

7. Prominent speaker(s) who may be a selling point

8. Registration information and deadlines

9. Contact names and telephone numbers for information

10. Adequate room for registrants to clearly write details

Programs with many aspects, speakers, and events will require more pages to get the message across completely. The registration form may be two pages long if participants are to register for multiple sessions and events.

A third consideration is how much impact the brochure must have to gain the attention of potential participants. If they regularly receive a number of multicolored and highly attractive brochures from your competitors, a plain piece won't stand out. Then again, maybe it will if its design and approach are unique and in stark contrast to those of the competition. Do not cheat on "your image." Even those who don't register for your program will remember the image it created and may come to another of your programs.

The number of brochures to be printed and how much money will have to be spent on mailing lists are the fourth consideration. In addition, you have to factor in the reliability of mailing lists. Old mailing lists lead to wasted postage and brochures. In determining the cost of mailings, figure in the number of follow-up mailings that will be necessary.

Lauffer (1978) reminds us of the importance of segmenting the market so that those who receive brochures and other marketing information are the ones most likely to be interested in the program. That segmenting, of course, is made easier when the concept of the program is clear and the audience for it equally so. Kowalski (1988) makes the point that if the program is designed to bring about social or other change than it is important to have the most appropriate participants, not just people to fill seats. You must identify who those participants will be. Increasingly, you will find brochures that contain information on "who should attend this program." Sending brochures to groups or organizations who do not have an interest in your current offerings may lead to negative marketing. That is, when a brochure for an appropriate program is received, it may automatically go the way of the others!

Another important marketing strategy is the use of incentives (Beder, 1986). Incentives are tangible items similar to souvenirs of the program such as pens, stationery, and mugs. They may also be in the form of group discounts, early bird registrations or package deals on the educational aspects, meals and social events. In preparing your budget these items must be figured into your cost structure. There is a temptation to be a little reckless when considering the large variety of mementos which are now available. Remember that an oversupply of these tangible items may be a complete write-off. It is better to be conservative in ordering and use the fact that there is a limited supply as a part of the marketing strategy.

Other incentives which can be used in marketing the program include special air fares arranged with airlines, accommodation packages arranged with hotels, and special discounts on local attractions. These will not figure into the budget, unless included as part of the program, but can be effective in helping potential participants budget for their attendance.

A final consideration is the availability and value of other marketing sources. Can the local media be used effectively to market a program? Will an advertisement in a regional publication produce results? What role does personal contact with potential participants play? What journals would be appropriate? These options have to be weighed carefully. Brochures are an established method for marketing programs but are not the only method and others should be considered. A mix of methods which gives repeated exposure will bring the greatest rewards.

Consider these alternative ways a program can be marketed.

1. Single sheet flyers sent out by mail with limited information on the program and a detachable registration sheet

2. A cover letter mailed with a brochure and signed by a person familiar to those who will receive the material

3. A memo announcing the program and how to register for it (only for programs where those who will attend are a small and distinct group)

4. Advertisements on radio and television, either paid or as a public service announcement

5. Advertisements in daily or weekly newspapers, including specialized ones in business or the professions, containing information about the program and a detachable registration sheet

6. Posters distributed throughout the target market area

7. Have this program announced at other programs where the audience may include potential participants

8. Personal contact with organizations whose employees would benefit from the program or with members of professional organizations

9. Trade and professional journals whose subscribers come from the target audience

These methods do work. Two drawbacks should be considered, however. First, most of them do not go to specific people. Second, tracking their impact can be difficult. You can ask participants how they heard about a program, if their enrollment is not from a brochure. This is a valuable source of information that is not always gathered.

An important aspect of marketing programs is the timeliness of the promotion. After deciding on the appropriate mix of promotional activities, you must establish a timeline for effecting the plan. How soon before the program should brochures be mailed? How long before a second mailing? For how long should registrations be held open?

In asking the questions about how much and what kind of marketing should be done, and when it should be done, Farlow (1979) suggests setting realistic expectations. Do not let the lure of grandiose publicity campaigns and advertising gimmicks overshadow the purpose of the program and the budget allocated to marketing. As the program planner, you must be in control of the marketing. We cannot stress enough the financial peril that accompanies the temptation to go overboard with publicity.

What Else Can Be Done to Market More Effectively

What we learn from out past marketing experiences is an important source of information to formulate and guide our marketing plan. Notes from previous renditions of the same or comparable programs are useful guides to what was done well or not. Past brochures can be examples of what to do again or avoid.

Past experience should also be used when determining how much marketing to do. Marketing is in the fixed cost column but does not necessarily remain static. Marketing efforts can quickly reach the point of diminishing returns, where continued efforts to reach more and more audiences fail to produce any measurable results. There is no formula that can be followed to identify when that point is reached. A number of factors described previously have to be weighed.

Finally, time and money can be spent on learning more about those who attend your program. Havlicek (1990) suggests building a data base with information about the sex, age, educational level, and participation history of those who have attended your programs. That information can be studied to learn more about similarities or differences in individual interests. Programs can be tailored to those interests. Conjecture and speculation are replaced by data.

Experience should tell intelligent planners that they can never avoid marketing a program, no matter how long it has been offered and how solid participant support appears to be. Marketing is most evident through the tangible items that participants receive to announce the program. But equally important marketing efforts occur through personal contacts participants have with program hosts before and during a program. In fact, every contact a participant has with program personnel is a marketing opportunity. Good and bad experience may well have far more impact than color or well-chosen words found on a brochure.

In all the material we have referred to in this section, the one theme which has prevailed is attention to customer service. Customer service should form the basis of all marketing activities. Two significant outcomes of excellence in customer service are word of mouth recruitment of new participants and retention of existing participants. "It is less expensive to keep a customer than to get a new one" (Coates & Dobmeyer, 1990, p. 18).

The cost of providing excellent customer service can be minimal and will initially involve training of volunteers and other members of the organization to better understand the needs and expectations of potential participants. Of course, the organization itself must be responsive and adaptive to customer needs and have a customer service orientation. Assessing the quality and effectiveness of customer service should be included in program evaluation, although it is often neglected.

One final thought on marketing. At what stage do you decide that your marketing is not generating sufficient interest to make the program viable and that you should not proceed with the program? There are no hard and fast rules, but experience will be one guide. The potential participant should also be considered. You must provide sufficient time for those who have already registered to cancel travel arrangements without penalty and rearrange schedules to make valuable use of this freed-up time. There are no guarantees, but a thoroughly developed budget and marketing plan will minimize the chances of having to make that decision.

SUMMARY

As with every other aspect of program planning, budgeting and marketing involve creativity and artistry. How much money is spent and in what ways, and the types of marketing done contribute to the program's image as much as the site or how learning activities are structured. A well-managed budget and attractive and effective marketing can guarantee continued association with cosponsors and those providing financial support to your programs. The impression of an efficient and professional operation contributes to the development and maintenance of loyalty among participants in your programs.

As we stated in Chapter 3 when we discussed collecting information on the "numbers," the budget is often the bottom line or at least the main guide to making decisions about proceeding with or abandoning programs. As much as we don't like to think this way in continuing education, it is a reality. The other reality is that marketing can be the one item which destroys the budget.

CHAPTER 6

Overseeing Details

All of us have social events we remember with awe. They could have been a wedding, a family reunion, or a community dinner. "How were the planners able to get all of this done?" you may have marveled. Every aspect of the event was without flaw. You left feeling very impressed and envious of the host's ability to plan, organize, and carry out such an elegant event.

You also will have memories concerning effective continuing education programs you attended. The educational activities and the people you met and had a chance to talk with are two parts of that memory. The details also play an important part in your memory. In fact, the little things could be as significant as the overall impression.

The sad truth, however, is that as program participants we remember the flaws and bad experiences of the event. Meals came late and were cold, the speaker was difficult to hear, sleeping rooms were not made up until late in the day, and there were insufficient handouts.

As a planner, your goal should be to create the educational programs that produce the cherished memories and minimize those incidents that sour participants' memories. Through the administrative and management areas to be covered in this chapter, you will learn more about how to do both. Remember, someone must take responsibility for overseeing all the details. Lenz (1980) reminds us that "in program presentation, there is no such thing . . . as an unimportant detail" (p. 70). It is attention to the little details as much as, or more than, the glamour of location or speakers that will set your successful program apart from the others.

In this chapter, the components of managing the event will

be identified and explained in detail. To begin, we ask "why the details?" and then consider a pessimistic view of what could happen. We will discuss the role of the host or the person in charge and then direct our attention to the site and what participants feel is basic to creature comfort. Do not forget that often we rely on volunteers to help with the operation of the event. Here we provide guidance on managing this valuable group of "workers." We give a brief discussion of a number of other details which require your attention prior to and during the program. The necessity for written confirmation and follow-up on arrangements is stressed. Finally, we address the importance of continuous oversight and conducting a final check before the program begins.

WHY THE DETAILS?

Those who plan and host effective events, regardless of what they are, share common characteristics. These will be explored later on in this chapter. Fundamental is a concern that the myriad of details associated with any educational program are managed and those responsible are pushed to be sure every facet of the event has been identified and will be handled in a complete and professional manner.

The stories of what can go wrong are legion. Even the most organized of planners can suggest what may seem to be unbelievable problems that even the most pessimistic of personalities would not have imagined. Those unexpected events have to be controlled before they become a crisis. Imagine planning a program only to discover shortly prior to the event that the major route to the venue was being repaired, causing major traffic tie-ups of 25 miles or longer. What do you do when you arrive at the venue only to discover that redecorating is in progress and the paint fumes and dust are throughout the building? What happens when another group using the venue is noisy, which affects the concentration of your participants.

Controlling the details of program presentation, because of the possibility of these horrors, is all the more important. First, attention to these matters puts emphasis on all the "little things" that contribute to a program's success. Planners and others involved focus on them, discuss the most logical approach, and remind each other of what must be done.

A second reason for an emphasis on details is the attention it brings to what could go wrong and the necessary back-up steps to take to prepare for that possibility. Alternative courses of action can be identified, for example, in case a room is not available or equipment breaks down. The details that must be addressed are discussed at length later in the chapter.

THE STARTING POINT— A PESSIMISTIC VIEW OF LIFE

Most continuing education programs are single events that are not part of a general routine. Detail and arrangement-related problems can become predictable and so be minimized in regularly held programs. To be sure, the unexpected occurs in public schools and colleges. Classes may be disrupted, but there is time to correct them and time to make sure material is covered. That isn't always possible with a one-day program, or even one occupying a week.

Experienced planners recognize this reality and consider what could go wrong to make this educational experience less than effective. Along with reviewing all details, they look at certain key areas that could produce difficulties immediately or in the future. These include but are not restricted to:

1. Critical contact and support personnel at hotels and other sites changes, requiring new relationships to be developed and details reviewed

2. Any changes in the facility where the program is to be held that could make the experience less satisfactory

3. Road construction or airline strikes, for example, that could make getting to and from the event more difficult

4. Unexpected delays in the arrival of needed materials and supplies

A central point is that you will be depending upon many people and organizations to get work done right, at the quality level desired and on time. Some may be volunteers. Others will be paid. Some care about what they are assigned to do, and others don't. You can't assume commitment and must operate with a "what could go wrong?" attitude.

With that attitude, you will allocate time and energy to follow up all those involved. Importantly, you will emphasize that your priority must become theirs and, in some cases that will be enough to get needed attention.

Files on past programs can provide clues to where problems may emerge. Pessimism and realism are connected here. What you think might happen and actually did happen come together. By checking memos and other records you are in a better position to think about what could go wrong. This is an excellent way to become prepared for these possibilities by developing a set of response options, and then to handle them more effectively. Not only should you be proactive in heading off potential problems, but you should be prepared to react quickly and rationally to problems as they surface.

A program must be led from its inception through its conclusion. When it actually takes place, some person must be the recognized leader or host of the event. Who will that person be?

The Host Role

"Who is in charge here? I have a question!"

This could be a complaint or a request for assistance. Participants do not want to be passed from person to person. An immediate response is expected, with an indication of what will be done. For programs of all sizes, this may be one of the most significant host functions performed. Participants want to know there is a knowledgeable person in a position of authority who has information, and can and will act. Dealing with these comments and suggestions and mixing with participants is very time consuming.

As you respond to participants' comments and suggestions, you can categorize them into four groups: (a) those that can be dealt with now, (b) those that can be used to correct the next program, (c) those that may be of benefit in the longer term, and (d) those that cannot be dealt with at all. Mixing with participants gives you an opportunity to gather feedback and to informally evaluate the proceedings. This is an important function as the program planner and the host.

A second important host role will be to welcome significant individuals including representatives of the cosponsors, speakers, and individuals whose support is essential to the program. This special recognition makes them feel good and adds another important touch to their experience with the program.

Related to this role can be opportunities to introduce people who have not met before and should. Individuals attend programs to learn, but another important reason is to meet and to see people. An astute planner can capitalize on an event to foster discussions that could have long-term value. Issues related to the program or other topics can be addressed.

The host should be the person to work with hotel and motel sales managers and others who control space. Changes may have to be made, and only one person should be responsible for negotiating changes. If extra money is to be spent on unforeseen items, that is another host duty.

Depending on where the program is held, it may be wise to meet briefly with the person in charge of the site. This could be a brief conversation to point out that the person in charge has arrived. In some cases, it will be the time to make sure staff is available to move in material and equipment. A very experienced program planner uses this period to meet the bell staff in hotels, tip them before any work is done, and remind them of more to come, if prompt and excellent service is provided.

Finally, effective planners will make sure there are enough people to assist with host duties. Depending upon the size of the program and the number of participants, several people may be needed to walk up to those with a confused look on their face, to clarify possibly confusing directions, and to explain what participants should do first. In some situations, assistance may be needed for those whose ability to speak and understand English is limited. The facility may be large and not well-marked. Any number of reasons may make it necessary to have many hosts so that participants begin the experience feeling they are being cared for by staff readily available to assist them.

A Critical Look at the Site

The site should be considered from seven different perspectives and all of the details within each perspective carefully evaluated. If you are thorough in evaluating the site, an important step has been taken to make this educational experience one that will be remembered with great fondness. Importantly, progress has been made in securing a market by choosing an attractive site. Your evaluation should include

- How the site contributes to the program goals. Consider the fit between the program and the site. Is it suitably formal or informal for the kinds of learning activities that will take place? Will participants be able to relax and separate themselves from routine responsibility to benefit from the event? The site should be one that allows, indeed promotes, interaction and exchange between participants.
- Participants' comfort level. You must ask yourself how comfortable participants will feel at this location. Will they feel at home or constantly wonder why this location was chosen? Comley (1990) suggests that a setting has to be created that makes participants feel they are welcome and have come to a "sanctuary" where they can be in an atmosphere conducive to learning. The hospitality of the service personnel contribute to this sanctuary.
- Distractions participants will face. In some cases, distractions can be a selling point and time for them is included in the program (a beach or ski slope, for example). You have to consider, however, if their attractiveness will have an impact on attendance at various program events. In some cases, a pool, a beach, walking trails, a nearby shopping mall or an interesting downtown area enable participants to get away briefly from the intensity of the program, especially if some participants see the program as an extension of their work. Friends from afar have a chance to relax together and valuable informal discussions take place.

- Physical comfort. You must pay attention to the details associated with accommodation and meeting rooms and how comfortable they are for participants. An important consideration is whether the location is large and arranged in a fashion that could confuse participants. Participants should not have battles to face; that is, long walks to rooms, hearing difficulties, keeping cool or warm. A program setting will be a new environment to participants, and you want to make the period of adjustment to it as short and as trauma free as possible.
- Amenities that add to the location's attractiveness. Given the emphasis on physical health, a gym, running track, or swimming pool might be features that will increase participant interest in attending a program. A tranquil locale offering opportunities for quiet reflection will be attractive to some groups. Others may want a bustling location that is a contrast from where they normally live and work.
- Site cost. Is it worth the money to hold the program at this location? Will participants feel that the cost is too high or, by contrast, that a more comfortable and costly location should have been sought? Some groups want to feel they have had an educationally successful meeting at a site with basic accommodations. Another group may want a wet bar in each room, because social events are a tradition. You should take into account who will actually be paying the registration fee. If the individuals have to fund it themselves, they may want economy.
- Reputation of the site. Is the site so well known that holding an event there will increase attendance? Does it have features that make it especially attractive for your group? Many groups are so used to being at the same site that its name is included in the program title. Tradition plays a role, especially when the same people return each year and look forward to being at a location that evokes such fond memories.

Overall, you want to look at the fit between the site and participants. Some groups return to the same location year after year because they relate past positive experience to both the content and to the site. However, regardless of whether the group is at the location for the tenth time or the first time, you must examine the site in light of each of these perspectives.

Sleep, Food, Productivity and Happy Participants

Another set of details you must be concerned with includes sleeping accommodations and meals for participants. Both should be appropriate to the group and contribute to a totally enjoyable experience. What you do not want to see are individuals who look tired and unhappy in the morning because their beds were uncomfortable and only lukewarm water was available. What you absolutely do not want to hear are criticisms of food because of what was prepared or how it was prepared.

Past experience should guide how you select a site where participants will remain overnight. Some locations would be suitable for a program of any length of time. In others, two or three nights is as long as participants will tolerate because accommodations are marginal.

Ask these questions as you consider the choice of accommodation.

- Will all accommodation be at the event site or are other facilities available within a reasonable distance?
- Will reservations for accommodation be handled by the planning committee or directly by the facility?
- What types of sleeping rooms are available? Are rooms available at various levels of cost and comfort? Does the advance registration form ask for accommodation preferences?
- What amenities are provided in the rooms?
- What extra amenities including recreation facilities are available?
- What is the policy for check-in and check-out times and for cancellations?
- Is the facility close to commercial and retail outlets? Is there an excessive noise problem from a nearby airport or freeways?

Today people are more conscious about what they eat. With some groups, food is an exceptionally important part of any program. You may be required to include certain items on your menu and avoid others. Special meal requests can be included in your preregistration form.

Ask these questions as you plan meals and menus.

- How many and what type of breaks will be needed?
- What refreshments will be served during these breaks?
- What meal breaks will be needed during the program?
- How extensive will the menus be for the meals?
- Will all meals be included in the registration fee or will participants be able to select those they wish to attend?
- Are any banquets or receptions planned? Who will be invited?
- Does the preregistration form ask for special dietary needs?
- How many complimentary meals will be provided and to whom?
- Will companions be invited to the meals and banquets?
- Will alcoholic beverages be served? Are special licenses required?
- What policy does the facility have for guaranteeing meal numbers?
- Will the function rooms require special set up, decorations, floral arrangements or special equipment?
- Are there nearby food outlets where participants can obtain meals independent of the program meals?

Taking Care of Volunteers

Integral to many continuing education programs, and especially in the actual conduct of the program, is a team of volunteers who will provide a great deal of support to the planning committee. We have spoken of the need for a number of hosts who may be needed to meet and greet participants and speakers, provide directions, and attend to the many tasks of keeping the program running. These people will more than likely be volunteers. They might be members of a cosponsoring organization or volunteer their time so that nonprofit programs can be offered to other members of their community.

Volunteers offer their services without consideration of being paid. However, as Malone and Gingera (1989) remind us, volunteers are not a free resource. There will be costs associated with meals, perhaps reduced registration fees if they are also participants, liability coverage, small gifts of recognition, and importantly, your time devoted to managing and directing the group.

Managing volunteers adds to your list of duties. There are a number of components involved in managing volunteers. These are identification, selection, recruitment, orientation, training, supervision, and recognition (Malone & Gingera, 1989). In some situations, volunteers will be self-identified and self-selected. You may have to be very careful in these situations so as not to take on unsuitable volunteers or in other situations not to offend those who you do not select.

No matter under what circumstances you select your volunteers, you must still orient them to their tasks and provide supervision. Supervision means getting the volunteers to successfully do those things you have assigned them (Wilson, 1976). They will require your support, encouragement, and guidance. Also, do not be afraid to listen to their suggestions.They are often closer to the action than you are and may provide valuable insight to improve the operation of the event.

Recognition of your volunteers is very important. Self-satisfaction and recognition are often the only positive outcomes people get from volunteering. Recognition provides positive reinforcement that encourages them to help out in the future (Malone and Ginera, 1989). There is no particular form of recognition that suits every occasion, but it may be sufficient to acknowledge them in the program or during the closing session. Alternatively you may choose a letter of appreciation, a certificate or plaque, or some small gift.

Remember, a volunteer's time may be free, but there is a cost in financial terms which you must account for in your budget and a cost in your time for training and supervision.

Other Details

Depending on the program topic, its format, location, and size, many tasks have to be accomplished prior to and during the program. In this section we bring some of these to your attention. Included are checklists which should provide some guidance as you take care of these details. We cannot possibly include every little step you should take, but by making you aware of these tasks we hope you will begin to ask questions of yourself and others about how to best deal with the many details of the program.

Registration Process

The registration process may begin several months prior to the program. This will be done by using a form attached to the promotional brochure. However, you must have a system for tracking registrations and having the materials available upon the participants' arrival at the site. At the site you must have a system for handling preregistrations and on-site registration. Many questions will arise during this process, and you may need a separate information table. Preparation of participant registration packets prior to the on-site registration will save much time and confusion.

Ask these questions as you plan the registration process.

- What are the procedures for preregistration?
- What are the procedures for on-site registration?
- What details will be included on the registration form?
- Who will staff the registration and information desks?
- How will registration records be maintained on-site?
- Will registration packets be assembled prior to the event?
- How will companion registrations be handled?
- How will presenter and exhibitor registrations be handled?
- How are cash, checks, and credit card receipts handled on-site?

Registration Packet

As participants register, they will expect to receive information on the program. The packet may be as elaborate as a satchel or portfolio embossed with the program name or as simple as a folder with a pocket on the inside. At the least, you should include a program and schedule of events, a name tag, details about the facility, "house keeping" details, and perhaps an evaluation form. Advertising material for local facilities or for the products of sponsors may be included.

Ask these questions as you plan the registration packet.

- What type of portfolio or folder will be used?
- What program materials will be included?
- Who will write a letter of welcome to be included in the packet?
- What advertising material from sponsors will be permitted?
- What code system will be used for name tags to distinguish between participants, hosts, presenters, and exhibitors?
- What promotional material or souvenirs will be included?
- Who will assemble the packets?
- Has the cost of the packets been included in the budget?

Program Materials and Proceedings

Presenters may ask you to provide copies of their presentations or worksheets for participants to become involved in the presentation. A workbook may be compiled for participants to complete reading assignments or to do exercises. This will depend on the format, the learning activity, and the presenter.

At the completion of the program you may compile a set of proceedings which includes all the presentations. This can often be a very time consuming and expensive exercise. It should be figured into the budget, if the proceedings are to be included with the registration fee. They might also be sold separately to nonparticipants.

Ask these questions as you plan program materials and proceedings.

- What materials will be prepared for participants?
- Have presenters been asked to supply material for distribution?
- Has the cost of copying material been included in the budget?
- Will proceedings be prepared after the program?
- What will it cost to prepare the proceedings?
- Will the proceedings be sold or included in the registration fee?
- Who will be responsible for recording or collecting the material?
- Who will assemble and edit the proceedings?

Equipment

You will need to have on hand a variety of equipment for most programs. Presenters may use simple teaching aids such as white boards, flip charts, and overhead projectors, or they may use video and audio equipment and computer assisted instruction. When providing this equipment, ensure that the accompanying tools are supplied such as pens, paper, and screens. Where electrical equipment is needed, check the room to ensure there are sufficient outlets.

The cosponsors may request that the program be videotaped or recorded. This requires extra time to set up and someone to operate or monitor the equipment. Respect the wishes of the presenters who do not want to be recorded. Collect information on equipment requirements and recording approval at the time the presenter agrees to participate.

Ask these questions when considering equipment requirements.

- What equipment is required for the program?
- Have the presenters indicated their equipment needs?
- Does the site facility have the necessary equipment?
- Where can equipment be rented if necessary?
- Are the rooms configured for using the equipment?
- Has the rental of equipment been included in the budget?

Special Needs Persons

Among the participants, companions, and presenters you may have persons who require special assistance. Laws now require many facilities to be equipped to accommodate people with special needs. These people include the blind, who may have a guide dog, the deaf, requiring you to provide a signer, and wheelchair bound participants requiring special access to rooms. If the program involves an overnight stay, special accommodations may be required.

Some participants may have special meal requirements. Consider the needs of elderly participants in planning your program. Perhaps alternative activities may be required. Information regarding these special needs can be collected on the registration forms. You should advise hosts that special needs participants will be in attendance and prepare the hosts for dealing with them. Also presenters may need to be advised so they can make accommodations in their presentations.

Ask these questions as you consider special needs persons.

- Does the registration form ask participants to list special needs?
- Does the site provide access and facilities for wheelchairs?
- Are signers required for those with hearing impairments?
- Are accommodations available for special needs participants?
- Does the site have facilities for guide dogs?
- Can the facility accommodate special meal requirements?
- Are presenters aware of the presence of special needs participants?
- Are there budget implications for providing for special needs?

Companion Activities

Companions are those people accompanying participants to the program. You must establish a policy on how companions will be involved. Some programs allow them to attend educational sessions only if they pay a registration fee. Others only include them in the social activities. Generally they will be registered along with the participant. You may be required to provide some additional activities for companions, although many accompany the participant with their own agenda of business or pleasure. Organizing activities for companions involves extra planning, additional registration work, and budgeting. However, these activities may prove to be a marketing incentive.

Ask these questions when planning companion activities.

- What is the policy for companion registrations?
- What program sessions will companions be permitted to attend?
- How will a registration fee be calculated for companions?
- Are separate activities to be planned for companions?

Exhibitions

For many large programs such as an annual conference, suppliers of products and services associated with the sponsoring organizations or the program topic may wish to publicize their goods and services through an exhibition. This is a major undertaking in itself and quite apart from the program. The decision to hold an exhibition in conjunction with the program should be carefully considered in light of its contribution to the goals of the program. It should be made early in the planning because of the impact it will have on the decisions of a number of variables including program sites, sponsorship, and budgeting. It may be a source of funding for the program.

Ask these questions when planning exhibitions.

- Will an exhibition be a part of this program?
- How does the exhibit contribute to the program goals?
- How many exhibitors will be invited and who?
- Will exhibitors be permitted to sell goods and services?
- What are the financial arrangements for the exhibition?
- Who will be responsible for setting up the exhibits?

Entertainment and Social Activities

Activities at which participants can relax and meet with colleagues in a less formal environment are considered very important by many program participants. As the program planner you have to decide what entertainment and social activities would be appropriate for this group. A poor choice of entertainment can be the cause of much unhappiness among participants. Sometimes entertainment can be combined with a learning activity. The other important consideration is the cost involved with hiring entertainers. This is a fixed expense which will have to be met. Entertainers may also require special attention which may place a strain on hosts and budgets.

Ask these questions as you plan entertainment and social activities.

- What entertainment and social activities will be included?
- How will these activities be used to enhance the program goals?
- Will the events be budgeted into the registration fee?
- Who will be responsible for coordinating the events?
- What local entertainment or attractions can be incorporated?
- What special requirements will be necessary for the entertainers?

Miscellaneous Details

There are many details which we may have failed to mention here. Each program and each site will present their own special needs and may require a great deal of attention. They may include:

- Setting up temporary office facilities at the program site with appropriate communications facilities
- Equipment for emergency photocopying and printing
- On-site assistance needed from the conference center or hotel to make sure all rooms are clean and arranged in appropriate formats
- On-site service personnel to attend to equipment failure, and problems which may arise with, for example, lighting, air conditioning, and heating
- Provision of transport for speakers or participants if the location is inaccessible by public transport, or simply as a courtesy
- Facilities for receiving messages for participants
- Telephones for participants
- Providing facilities for the press if they are invited
- Availability of emergency medical assistance
- The need for security if prominent persons are invited
- Provision of a hospitality suite for speakers, special guests, or cosponsors
- Abiding by regulations on smoking in facilities and designating areas for smokers to use if necessary

THE IMPORTANCE OF WRITTEN CONFIRMATION

Depending upon the complexity of the program, you may be working with a number of individuals and organizations. Each of them will have other responsibilities in addition to your needs. Your concerns might be a high priority for them at the time of your planning discussions about work to be completed. The importance of your needs could fade quickly once the discussions are complete. Written agreements are often needed which set out the expectations and responsibilities of the various parties involved. There are two types of agreements.

The first written agreement that is usually made is between the program planner and the sponsors or organizations who have contracted to develop, plan, and deliver the program. Appendix C is an example of a written agreement which sets out the expectations and responsibilities of the parties involved in planning a program. Other written agreements may be with individuals or organizations who provide various materials and services for the program.

Follow-up has been mentioned already in this chapter. Along with the pressure these reminders provide, written agreements make your expectations clear. Hotels, motels, conference centers, and other meeting facilities require them. Details are especially important where facilities, food, and the amenities that go along with both are concerned. In a large hotel with separate departments for meeting rooms, housekeeping, and food, your request will go to different supervisors. What you want must be clear to each of them. Orders for special material to be prepared and cost estimates for producing brochures are also made as written agreements. Confirmation letters can be prepared for speakers, outlining both their responsibilities to the program and your responsibilities to the speaker.

These written documents are valuable for at least two reasons. First, you are forced to write down details and to search your mind to be sure that none are forgotten. It provides a valuable reference document in your planning and for future planning.

The second reason agreements are valuable is the protection they provide you in a case where your requests have not been met. Even though these are legal documents, there is no guarantee of success. You are however, in a far stronger position with an agreement. If the requests agreed to cannot be met, then you can use the agreement as the basis, for example, for refusing to pay for certain charges, or you can diplomatically but firmly request that a site manager do what had been agreed to in the contract. This occurs with far more regularity than might be imagined, and reductions in bills are negotiated.

If the situation is serious, then legal action may be warranted to seek compensation. The situation may also arise where you are at fault. For example, if you agree on a set number of meals and the registrations are lower than you budgeted, you will be responsible for the cost of the unused meals. These situations can be avoided by careful attention to the budget, notification deadlines, and margins for flexibility.

CONTINUOUS OVERSIGHT

At the same time that you are handling program-related details, you should also be monitoring three other important areas:

- the program's finances
- how well deadlines are being met
- the happiness of cosponsors and the way cooperative relationships are being built

In fact, this monitoring function is part of the overall program evaluation and is an effective way of spotting potential problems at an early stage.

As registration forms and fees are received and money is spent, the overall spending pattern should be monitored. With computerization of financial management, producing reports has become very easy. It is possible to look at: the comparison between income and expense; how rapidly or slowly registrations are coming in; if there are any unusual expenses; or if costs are higher in particular areas than were anticipated.

How well deadlines are being met should be a next concern. Are speakers providing material they want duplicated in a timely fashion? Is other information coming in as requested? Is the site providing menu and housing information you need? This information will alert you to what work may have to be done at the last minute and the kind of extra help you may need to get it done.

Finally, happiness should be a concern. Cosponsors should be kept aware of what is going on and any of their questions or concerns should be addressed. They may have useful suggestions for changes or can intervene to get material or move a process along faster. Those cosponsors unfamiliar with the planning and management necessary to produce these one-time educational programs can be complacent or very worried or at some point in between the two. Regardless of how they feel, keeping them informed is a courtesy, an essential element in strengthening a relationship, and an intelligent way to get useful assistance.

Participants arrive with a variety of expectations and intentions. One speaker may be the reason for attending, or the mix of people could be the main attraction. You can't have much of a direct impact on what brought them to this program, but you can do a great deal to provide them with a great memory of this event. Although the program is in place and will take on a life of its own once events begin, you continue to play an important role in four very important areas:

- as a host
- as the manager of details
- as the monitor of relationships
- as the leader of informal evaluation

IS EVERYTHING IN PLACE?

Anyone in charge of an event will be nervous about all things being in place at the right time. Today, because service attitudes have declined in many places, attention to the setting and everything within it is critical. A walk-through to check to see that all rooms have been set up as requested is a basic task. Related to this step can be a review with site staff to make sure they handle changes in room arrangements or special events that will require attention. There is a turnover in staff at these facilities, and so your request may be new to those who actually do the work.

Through the walk-through and other contacts, you can identify what might go wrong. If this event is a repeat, you can look back to see if any unfortunate incidents could occur again. Some of the details you can check on as you walk through the facility include:

- The appropriate room arrangements with chairs and tables are set up to suit the particular program format.
- Audiovisual equipment is set up and working.
- All refreshments available during the sessions and breaks are set up.
- Any temporary distractions such as cleaners or minor repairs will be complete prior to the start of the program.
- Any special displays or decorations are in place.
- Handout materials are available where participants will see them.

If you discover that things are not all in order as you had requested, you may find that you can rectify the situation faster yourself than waiting for the facility's personnel to make the changes.

Depending on the size and complexity of the program, any number of problems can arise. You need to constantly visualize what things might occur and be prepared to take action as quickly as possible. By making simple reminders to the appropriate personnel, you can often avert trouble.

AN EVALUATION POINT

The planners and others concerned with the success of the event can begin to gather information that will become part of the program's evaluation. What can be evaluated at this point? Consider the following:

- How easily participants are able to move into and around the facility
- How quickly and efficiently the registration process was completed
- How well prepared the site hosts appeared to be for the event
- What participants were saying as they entered that could provide a clue to their attitude as the event begins

Information should be gathered quickly and changes made with the same rapidity. You can apologize if a change isn't possible. Your notes should be in the program file so that any mistakes are not repeated.

SUMMARY

There are many details which must be attended to throughout the planning and conduct of a continuing education program. Attention to the details in the initial planning process will help make the program run smoothly. However, as we have said, there are any number of little challenges which can arise which will require prompt and appropriate action. Being prepared is the best way of dealing with those challenges. Making checklists and asking questions similar to those we have provided is a excellent way of avoiding many problems and being prepared for those which do arise.

CHAPTER 7

Wrapping Up the Program and Planning for the Future

The program is over but should not be forgotten quickly. There are required tasks that must be completed and others that should be done, if this program is going to have an impact on future activities. Three required activities to be addressed in this chapter are the financial review, indications of appreciation and reaction, and the final program evaluation. Other activities include an evaluation summary and program manager report to the planning committee, the assembly of files for possible future use, follow-up contacts with speakers and others who contributed to the program, and discussions about the next programs.

All of these activities are important, but could be called the mechanical dimensions. They must be done. To what extent they are done will depend upon the program's complexity, reporting requirements that may exist, and how much time is available.

A second activity enables you to learn from this experience. As was mentioned earlier, those who don't study the past will not benefit from the valuable lessons it can provide. In the second section of this chapter, we will suggest the kinds of questions that can be raised and what kinds of thought can be given to what has been learned from this program experience.

During all the phases of program development and operation you must manage process, content, and politics at the same time. That requires a form of creativity and, indeed, artistry, which is developed through experience and reflection. Throughout this book, we have suggested how all three of these elements must be managed. In this final chapter, two additional elements will be examined: how to bring a program to a close in a complete and careful way, and how to find time to learn from the program just completed.

FOCUS ON THE MECHANICS

A program is not concluded until the activities described in this section are addressed. You and others associated with the program will be tired after participants leave. Rightly so. A lot of effort has been devoted to creating a successful educational experience.

Take some time to relax, and then focus your attention on getting the following done. Some are essential, the financial review for example. The others show that you have taken this program seriously, and you appreciate the efforts others have made to make this program a successful one. Don't forget them!

Financial Review

This is a must activity, regardless of the size of the program and its budget. The first step is to ensure that all accounts are paid and paid promptly. Promptness in settling accounts is one way of creating a positive image with those who supply goods and services. Especially important is to promptly pay the speakers and presenters. They may have been paid at the conclusion of their presentation. Your attention to their compensation will be in your favor should you call on them for future programs.

Bills may come in slowly, and it may be weeks, even months, before you will be able to do a complete review of revenue and expenses. Once all of the bills have been paid and recorded, a final financial report can be prepared. A quick review of the report should highlight the major expenses and to what extent they were different from those that were anticipated.

You can supply information of this kind to all of those on the planning committee. Obviously, when income and expenses are nearly equal or there is a profit, this information is an indication of a well-planned and well-managed program. The financial report may not be an indication of a successful program, since success is measured by a number of criteria.

You should pay special attention to areas with a significant difference between projected and actual costs. Most importantly is to understand why that happened. Jot down the answer with your report to be used for future reference. That information is money saved or money made, or both!

Indications of Appreciation and Reaction

Saying "thank you" in a timely fashion is a habit that true professional program planners demonstrate. Letters of thanks and commendation, along with gifts when appropriate, should be sent out as soon as possible. Thank everyone and personalize those letters as much as possible. The managers of those who have helped out should be sent copies of those letters.

All who have contributed will appreciate being recognized, even if they are to receive payment for their efforts. In some cases, news releases are written to announce an individual's participation in a program. There are creative ways to say thanks, including providing books or art work. Some individuals cannot receive payment, but a gift to their organization will be accepted and appreciated.

There will be programs where the planner is not completely satisfied with certain aspects. When, for example, the site, meals, or material prepared were not what was promised, it is important to make that clear. A letter stating clearly the shortcomings is appropriate. Participant evaluations can be used to support your grievances. Remember you have a letter of agreement which outlines exactly what was expected. A letter can produce results that may include a reduction in charges if what was not done was significant and had a direct impact on the program. Those who provide services are anxious to please and look closely at complaints.

Summative Evaluation

All of the informal evaluation material along with information collected from participants can be joined together in a final evaluation. Participant reactions are very important but not always easy to obtain; shorter evaluations with more forced-choice options may be more attractive than longer and more detailed ones. Figure 7.1 is a sample of evaluation questions in three different formats which can be adapted to suit your program. This type of evaluation is designed to capture participant's immediate reactions to the just completed program.

Responses to open-ended questions can be used in future marketing material. The participants should be identified by name and give their approval to their names and comments appearing on marketing material.

An important question to answer when evaluations are developed is: "How much information about which program aspects should be gathered?" For example, a program that has been offered successfully for four consecutive years may not require such an extensive examination. Attention could be limited to new aspects of the program or an area that was rated low in the past and has been changed.

Increasingly, program planners ask those who speak or participate in other ways to complete an evaluation. These evaluations obtain reactions to their experience with the program, particularly how they were provided with information prior to the program and how they were treated during the program.

Evaluation summaries are a guide to what should be changed and what portions of the program must be maintained as they are. When participant comments are used, they can be thanked for their help and reminded that their help figured in the planning for the next program.

Additional Activities

There are a number of additional activities that can be completed, depending upon the program and who was involved in it.

Program Summary and Report

This summary could be prepared for the planning committee and others involved in the program. In addition to a review of what happened and an evaluation summary, details of the planning process, difficulties experienced, and lessons learned could be included. This report will form the basis of your formal

Figure 7.1 Sample summative evaluation questions

CLOSED QUESTIONS USING SCALES

Please circle your response

1. Overall, how beneficial was the program?

   Of no benefit   Very Beneficial

   1   2   3   4   5

2. How would you rate the quality of instruction?

   Poor   Excellent

   1   2   3   4   5

3. The length of the program was:

   Too long   About right   Too short

   1   2   3   4   5

4. The amount of material covered was:

   Too little   About right   Too much

   1   2   3   4   5

5. The program fulfilled its stated objectives.

   Strongly disagree   Strongly agree

   1   2   3   4   5

6. Rate the program site and facilities.

   Unsatisfactory   Satisfactory

   1   2   3   4   5

RATING GROUP ITEMS

Please evaluate the following sections by circling your response on the rating scale.

	Poor		Satisfactory		Excellent

Educational aspects:

	Poor		Satisfactory		Excellent
• Program content	1	2	3	4	5
• Program format	1	2	3	4	5
• Program book	1	2	3	4	5
• Handouts	1	2	3	4	5
• Presenters	1	2	3	4	5
• Instruction methods	1	2	3	4	5

Program site and facilities:

	Poor		Satisfactory		Excellent
• Registration process	1	2	3	4	5
• Site facilities	1	2	3	4	5
• Meals	1	2	3	4	5

OPEN-ENDED QUESTIONS

How will you apply what you have learned?

What are the strengths of this program?

In what ways could the program be improved?

request to obtain additional funding or support for future programs from the various cosponsors. It will also be the basis of an accountability report to current cosponsors. In certain cases the cosponsors may have a set format for preparing a report.

Capturing Essential Details

Various details can be captured so that planners can benefit if this or a similar program is held in the future. These details may include who to contact regarding special arrangements such as renting buses, how special permits are obtained, and what companies can do certain specialized duplicating work. That list can be stored in the files to be used again when the program is next planned. A complementary list could be made of what to do or not to do the next time. You should also establish a file where information is kept on specific topics including transportation, duplicating and printing services, accommodations, equipment rental, and security services. Another file might include standard letters and forms, including evaluation forms, which can be adapted for each program. These two can be revised as the result of program evaluations.

Follow-Up Evaluation

A follow-up evaluation can be considered in some cases, especially when there is great interest in how participants have applied what they have learned. For example, a group of teachers may have been provided with guides to incorporating material on AIDS into their curriculum, and the sponsors want to know what actually was adopted. Asking all participants or a cross section of them is a useful activity. It is also an indication to the participants that you have a continuing interest in them and the program.

Decisions About the Next Set of Programs

While motivation is high and information about what happened is current, the planners can discuss a follow-up session, the next annual event, or other topics that can be considered. Often with annual programs, the members of the sponsoring organizations choose future locations, times, and themes for future programs far in advance. Any input you have to inform their decision will make your task easier. You will also have begun to work on building those all important relationships.

LEARNING FROM HISTORY

Time should be set aside for you to take a step back and reflect on what you have learned. This learning is designed to identify what you do well and in what specific ways you should improve. Should your detail management skills improve? In what ways could your budget development be more precise? Could you do a better job working with the planning committee?

Only when you study your performance immediately after a program will you be able to identify necessary improvement. Then you can identify habits that caused problems and make a commitment to lessen their impact. Every program you plan should be a learning experience for you.

You can also learn from this review the things that made this program easy or difficult to develop and manage. Ask questions such as: Was it the topic or the type of people who attended the program? What advantages or difficulties did the site present? Were there people who helped you who made special contributions or did some of them make life unbearable?

Through these questions, you can determine the "hassle" level of this program. If you must be responsible for planning it in the future , answers to these questions will prepare you to run the program with less difficulty. If you have the option to continue or not continue it, the answers will help you make this decision.

No program is an event unto itself, with no history or future. Programs can provide an experience that leads cosponsors to want to work together again. You should look at this dimension of the experience. Would you want to work with the same cosponsors again? What changes would you make in the group? How would you operate differently with that group?

The program may have led you to consider other programs to offer. What would they be and who would they serve? How soon do you want to become involved in them?

Finally, you want to consider the strength of the structure you have created to plan the program. This is especially important if you plan a great many programs. Does that structure smooth the planning process but allow you enough flexibility to adapt to special situations?

In conclusion, you might wish to consider these questions as you reflect on the program and your role as a program planner.

- What have I learned about these participants that will enable me to serve them better in the future?
- What have I learned about the ease or difficulty of planning this program that will be valuable in the future?
- What kind of advice will I need in the future and from whom?
- Can the program be changed? In what ways? Can its boundaries be expanded to include new and risky activities and events?
- Should it be done again? Why? When?
- How could more people be attracted? To attract more people would educational quality or ethical standards need to be sacrificed in any way?
- Can the financial management be improved? How?
- Could the program itself be better managed to make the total experience a better one for the participants?
- Can we learn more from participants through our evaluation?
- What new technology may be incorporated to improve the management and delivery of the program?
- Overall, can my creativity be applied in more constructive ways? Can artistry make the event a better one?
- What have I learned about my ability as a planner, and in what ways do I have to improve?

PERSONAL REFLECTION

Consider this last question again. What have I learned about my ability as a planner and in what ways do I have to improve?

Expand the scope of the question. What have I learned? This question is very important for your own personal and professional growth as a continuing educator. As we are constantly pressured to deliver great programs for our many audiences, we often overlook our own needs to continue learning. Take time to reflect on each program and its contribution to your own development.

Depending on the situation, you can meet with others or with someone in your organization to discuss the program and what you have learned. A debriefing session can not only help with your professional growth but it may be an opportunity to air personal grievances or troubles that you faced through the program planning process. It is very important to have this time for yourself. This is not an evaluation of the program but more an analysis of your role as a program planner and your satisfaction with that role. In addition, attend other programs as a participant not only to see how others are doing it, but to learn for your own health and growth.

SUMMARY

Planning and operating credit programs is demanding, no matter how short or simple the program. An educational event apart from the routine of most of those involved must be created so that what it intends to accomplish is clear and all of the many details associated with it have been identified and handled.

Throughout this book, we have identified common tasks and challenges that must be addressed. Unlike some in our field, we have not suggested a model we feel will work in a great many situations. Rather we encourage you to look at each program planning situation as a unique one and adapt how it is managed to the particular topic and people involved.

Keep your eye on the process that must be completed if the program is to be planned in a timely fashion. Work hard to make sure that the educational content receives its proper emphasis. And finally, be sensitive to the political dimensions that will occur in every situation. All three must be managed simultaneously.

The results can be a memorable event for everyone involved. Participants learned. Informal activities were beneficial to many of those attending. The cosponsors had a successful experience and built what could prove to be an important working relationship.

As the program planner, you can take pride in moving an idea for a continuing education program to a reality. The many complex and unplanned challenges you faced were addressed in a professional way. Equally important, you learned just how much planning and energy is required to develop effective programs, and will be a better manager of these events in the future.

As we have mentioned earlier, this activity is not for the faint of heart. Continuing education remains an extremely important form of learning for a substantial number of individuals. By shaping your own philosophy and approach, you are better prepared to develop effective programs and enjoy the sense of achievement that this accomplishment deserves.

APPENDIX A

Planning Interview Worksheet

Individual Interviewed _____

Staff Member _____ Date_____

1. General Program Topic_____
2. Chief Program Contact_____
3. Principal Sponsor(s) _____
4. Secondary Sponsor(s)_____
   _____
5. Proposed Date(s) _____
   • Alternative Choices_____
6. Proposed Location_____
   • Alternative Choices_____
7. Basic Organization
   • Plenary Sessions _____
   • Break Out Sessions _____
   • Other activities _____
8. Major Speakers (Proposed Fee)
   •_____
   •_____
9. Panelists & Others Presenting (Proposed Fee)
   •_____
   •_____
   •_____
10. Food Service
    • Breakfast _____
    • Lunch _____
    • Dinner _____
    • Breaks _____
    • Social Events _____
11. Facilities Needed
    • Meetings _____
    • Meals & Functions _____
    • Sleeping Rooms _____
    • Other _____

12. Equipment Needed
    - Audiovisual _____
    - Other _____
13. Materials Provided to Participants at Registration
    - _____
14. Materials Provided During the Program
    - _____
15. Marketing Plans
    - Brochures_____
    - Free publicity _____
    - Paid Advertising _____
    - Other _____
16. Exhibitors
    - _____
17. Anticipated Income
    - By Source
        Grants _____
        Sponsors _____
        Fees _____
        Exhibitors _____
        Other _____
    - Fee Structure_____
18. Other Services
    - Transportation_____
    - Accommodation _____
    - Other _____
19. Miscellaneous Details
    - Press _____
    - Entertainment _____
    - Companion Activites _____
    - Other _____
20. Planning Timetable
    - _____
    - _____
    - _____
    - _____
    - _____

APPENDIX B

Program Formats and Learning Activities

Seminar

A seminar focuses on the study of a particular topic and requires involvement through discussion by all members of the group. It provides for detailed and systematic discussion and inquiry. The seminar leader is generally recognized as an expert in the topic and serves as a resource person and guides the discussion. The "instruction" remains the responsibility of the participants.

Forum, Symposium, and Panel

Although there may be subtle differences between these three formats, they essentially establish a setting where a number of points of view can be presented. There may be a panel of speakers who present their points of view, and audience members can react or present their own point of view.

Clinic

A clinic may focus on one particular problem and involve demonstration and practice of a particular skill or procedure. One or more experts are on hand to guide the practice.

Institute

The institute format is where a particular topic or skill is the focus of a number of intensive sessions over one or more days. A panel of experts may serve as instructors or resource people.

Workshop

A workshop is generally an intensive session devoted to the development of new skills, extension of knowledge, or development of ideas, a philosophy, or a mission among a group with common work-related experiences and knowledge. Often the group may break into pairs or subgroups to address issues and report back to the whole.

Course

The course format is for programs which meet for an extended period at regular intervals. It may be a short course that meets daily for a short time, or it may be a longer course which meets, for example, weekly for a full semester.

Lecture

A lecture is used where an authority or well known speaker delivers a talk or dissertation in a formal manner to an audience. It may be a part of series of lectures on a regular or ad hoc basis which address a particular issue(s) or topic of general interest to a particular audience.

Conference and Convention

A conference or convention is a large meeting of one or more days where participants gather to share knowledge, exchange information, learn from experts, and solve problems. Often the participants will belong to a common association, and the conference is an annual opportunity to conduct the association business as well as offer an educational event.

Field Trip and Field Day

Although these are quite distinct, they both have the objective of taking the participant to the site of the learning. Participants can see the topic under discussion in its real environment or in actual practice.

Study Tour

Study tours combine the elements of exploration, relaxation, adventure and learning in an extended "field trip." A great deal of planning and attention to detail is required, especially for foreign travel.

Exhibit

An exhibit may be held as a part of a conference or convention. Displays of products and processes are mounted to supplement other learning activities. Exhibits may have a commercial aspect to them in that products may be available for sale.

Poster Session

A poster session allows experts or people with new knowledge to share to prepare a "poster" display of their work and to be on hand to explain and answer questions.

Teleconference

Various forms of telecommunications can form the basis of an educational program. A teleconference links participants by audio or video or both, permitting participation without the expense of travel.

APPENDIX C

Written Agreement Between Program Planner and Program Sponsors

This document serves as an agreement between the Department of Secondary Education (DSE) and Conferences and Institutes (C&I) regarding the 67th Annual Education Conference, to be held December 1–3, 1994 at the Champaign Regent Hotel.

This agreement is intended to clearly define the expectations and responsibilities of the two parties. The signatures at the end of this agreement indicate the acceptance of those expectations and responsibilities by both parties.

1.   The attached budget is a part of this agreement.

The budget represents estimated costs and revenues. Actual costs and revenues may vary. When the actual cost of a budget line item appears likely to exceed the estimated amount by more that 10%, the expenditure will be discussed and mutually agreed upon between C&I and DSE.

C&I assumes no liability for any expenses which are incurred by DSE without C&I's prior knowledge and consent.

C&I will establish a revolving account for the express purpose of collecting revenues and disbursing expenses related to this conference. C&I will provide DSE with estimated financial statements on an interim basis, and a full accounting of revenues and expenses approximately 120 days following the close of the conference.

The registration fee of $96.00 per person has been set by DSE with the understanding that the actual per person cost will most likely exceed this amount. "Actual per person cost" is defined as the total of all expenses incurred in conjunction with the conference, divided by the number of people who actually attend the conference.

After all revenues and expenses have been accounted for, DSE will issue to C&I a grant equal to any resulting deficit. A 'deficit' is defined as the amount of money by which total revenues collected through registration fees falls short of total expenses for the conference.

C&I's administrative fee will be $7,000.00, regardless of the number of people who actually attend the conference.

2.   Refunds of registration fees.

It is C&I practice that registrants who cancel their registration prior to the start of a conference incur a 10% penalty, the balance being refunded. This practice will apply to this conference.

If the conference is cancelled for any reason whatsoever, including inclement weather, insufficient registrations, or any other circumstances, all registrants will receive a full refund.

If the conference is cancelled, regardless of the date of or reason for the cancellation, DSE will be liable for any and all expenses incurred to date, including hotel cancellation fees for meeting space, sleeping rooms, and meals, as well as all other expenditures incurred up to the time of cancellation.

3.   C&I will perform the following administrative tasks:

Make arrangements with the hotel regarding meeting space, blocking of sleeping rooms, meals, breaks, audiovisual equipment, and any other details necessary to provide the services and materials required by the conference. Registrants will make their own reservations for sleeping rooms, and are responsible for their own expenses.

Coordinate with DSE on the composition, production, and distribution of materials announcing the conference and promoting attendance. All materials are subject to DSE approval.

Establish a data base for the collection of registration data and the accounting of revenues from registration fees.

Acknowledge by letter all registrations, providing additional information regarding travel to the conference, sleeping accommodations, schedule information, and so on.

Collect all revenues and pay all expenses.

Contact speakers from a list provided by DSE and coordinate with them on the scheduling of their presentation, audiovisual equipment, printed materials, and other details related to their presentations.

Arrange for payment of honoraria to speakers along with agreed-upon travel and per diem expenses.

Assemble and distribute registration packets for participants, including name badges, programs, and other materials agreed upon between DSE and C&I. All materials are subject to DSE approval.

Provide an agenda of activities to take place during the conference, including the titles of presentations and the names of speakers.

Provide continuous on-site administration during the conference, including check-in/registration of participants and oversight of all other conference activities.

Other duties mutually agreed upon between C&I and DSE.

4.   DSE will perform the following administrative tasks:

Designate a single individual to represent DSE in all matters regarding the conference, with the authority to make decisions and approve expenditures. This person should be reasonably accessible throughout the planning phase, and continuously available for the duration of the conference itself.

Contact speakers and secure their agreement.

Provide information to and coordinate with C&I on the composition, production, and distribution of materials publicizing the conference and promoting attendance. C&I reserves the right of approval on all materials sent to potential participants, as well as those distributed at the conference.

Assist C&I in securing access to relevant data bases in order to establish mailing lists for publicity and promotion.

Other duties mutually agreed upon between the C&I and DSE.

....

John Black, Program Director   Date
Conferences and Institutes

....

Mary Martin, Chairperson   Date
Department of Secondary Education

BIBLIOGRAPHY

Apps, J.W . (1991). *Mastering the teaching of adults*. Malabar, FL: Krieger.

Aslanian, C. B., & Bricknell, H. M. (1980). *Americans in transition: Life changes as reasons for adult learning*. New York: College Entrance Examination Record.

Beatty, P. T., Benefield, L. L., & Linhart, L. J. (1991). Evaluating the teaching and learning process. In M. W. Galbraith (Ed.), *Facilitating adult learning: A transactional process* (pp. 163–192). Malabar, FL: Krieger.

Beder, H. W. (Ed.). (1984). *Realizing the potential of interorganizational cooperation*. New Directions for Continuing Education, no. 23. San Francisco: Jossey-Bass.

Beder, H. (1986). Basic concepts and principles of marketing. In H. Beder (Ed.), *Marketing continuing education.* (pp. 3–18). New Directions for Continuing Education, no. 31. San Francisco: Jossey-Bass.

Bennett, N. L., & LeGrand, B. F. (1990). *Developing continuing professional education programs* (The Guides Series in Continuing Education). Urbana-Champaign: University of Illinois at Urbana-Champaign.

Bennis, W., & Nanus, B. (1985). *Leaders: Strategies for taking charge*. New York: Harper & Row.

Boone, E. J. (1985). *Developing programs in adult education*. Englewood Cliffs, NJ: Prentice-Hall.

Boyle, P. G. (1981). *Planning better programs*. New York: McGraw-Hill.

Brookfield, S. D. (1986). *Understanding and facilitating adult learning*. San Francisco: Jossey-Bass.

Broomall, J. K., & Skwarek, R. (1991). The partnership model of program development: Meeting the needs of continuing higher education students. *Continuing Higher Education Review, 55*(3), 129–143.

Byers, P. Y., & Wilcox, J. R. (1991). Focus groups: A qualitative opportunity for researchers. *The Journal of Business Communications, 28*(1), 63–78.

Caffarella, R. S. (1988). *Program development and evaluation resource book for trainers.* New York: John Wiley & Sons.

Cervero, R. M. (1988). *Effective continuing education for professionals.* San Francisco: Jossey-Bass.

Cervero, R. M., & Wilson, A. L. (1994). *Planning responsibly for adult education: A guide to negotiating power and interests.* San Francisco: Jossey-Bass.

Charuhas, M. S. (1993). Utilizing unilateral and multilateral groups to enhance program development. In P. Mulcrone (Ed.), *Current perspectives on administration of adult education programs.* (pp. 45–56). New Directions for Adult and Continuing Education, no. 60. San Francisco: Jossey-Bass.

Chickering, A. W. (1971). *Experience and learning: An introduction to experiential learning.* New Rochelle, NY: Change Magazine Press.

Coates, J. & Dobmeyer, E. (1990). Ten trends in marketing adult and continuing education. *Adult Learning, 2*(1), 17–18.

Comley, R. E. (1990). Creating an atmosphere for the learning sanctuary. In E. G. Simpson & C. E. Kasworm (Eds.), *Revitalizing the residential conference center environment* (pp. 53–62). New Directions for Adult and Continuing Education, no. 46. San Francisco: Jossey-Bass.

Cote, L. S., & McAfee, J. K. (1987). Liability and risk management for continuing education professionals. *Continuing Higher Education Review, 51*(1), 1–14.

Cross, K. P. (1981). *Adults as learners.* San Francisco: Jossey-Bass.

Cranton, P. A. (1989). *Planning instruction for adult learners.* Toronto: Wall & Thompson.

Dahl, C. C. (1993). *Blending the roles of interpreter, entrepreneur, collaborator: A new model for conferences and institutes program planners* (The Guide Series in Continuing Education). Urbana-Champaign: University of Illinois at Urbana-Champaign.

Deshler, D. (Ed.). (1984). *Evaluation for program improvement.* New Directions for Continuing Education, no. 24. San Francisco: Jossey-Bass.

Donaldson, J. F. (1990). *Managing credit programs in continuing higher education* (The Guide Series in Continuing Education). Urbana-Champaign, IL: University of Illinois at Urbana-Champaign.

Falk, C. F. (1986). Promoting continuing education programs. In H. Beder (Ed.), *Marketing continuing education* (pp. 49–72). New Directions for Continuing Education, no. 31. San Francisco: Jossey-Bass.

Farlow, H (1979). *Publicizing and promoting programs.* New York: McGraw-Hill.

Galbraith, M. W. (1990). Attributes and skills of an adult educator. In M. W. Galbraith (Ed.), *Adult learning methods: A guide for effective instruction* (pp. 3–22). Malabar, FL: Krieger.

Galbraith, M. W. (Ed.) (1991). *Facilitating adult learning: A transactional process.* Malabar, FL: Krieger.

Griffith, W. S. (1989). Recruiting and retaining adult students: A marketing perspective. In P. S. Cookson (Ed.), *Recruiting and retaining adult students* (pp. 23–33). New Directions for Continuing Education, no. 41. San Francisco: Jossey-Bass.

Guba, E. G., & Lincoln, Y. S. (1981). *Effective evaluation.* San Francisco: Jossey-Bass.

Havlicek, C. (1990). Demystifying database marketing. *Adult Learning, 2*(1), 13–15.

Hiemstra, R (Ed). (1991). *Creating environments for effective adult learning.* New Directions for Adult and Continuing Education, no. 50. San Francisco: Jossey-Bass.

Hobbs, W. C. (Ed.). (1982). *Understanding academic laws.* New Directions for Institutional Advancement Series, no. 16. San Francisco: Jossey-Bass.

Houle, C. O. (1961). *The inquiring mind.* Madison, WI: University of Wisconsin Press.

Houle, C. O. (1972). *The design of education.* San Francisco: Jossey-Bass.

Jarvis, P. (1987). *Adult learning in the social context.* London: Croom Helm.

Kidd, J. R. (1973). *How adults learn.* Chicago: Follett.

Knowles, M.S. (1980). *The modern practice of adult education: From pedagogy to andragogy.* New York: Cambridge.

Knox, A. B. (1990). *Helping adults learn.* San Francisco: Jossey-Bass.

Knox, A. B. (1991). Educational leadership and program administration. In J. M. Peters, P. Jarvis & Associates, *Adult education: Evolution and achievements in a developing field of study* (pp. 217–258). San Francisco: Jossey-Bass.

Kolb, D. A. (1984). *Experiential learning: Experience as the source of learning and development.* Englewood Cliffs, NJ: Prentice-Hall.

Kowalski, T. J. (1988). *The organization and planning of adult education.* Albany, NY: State University of New York Press.

Kozoll, C. E. (1980). *The planning committee: When and how to use one* (Readings in Program Development, No. 3). Urbana-Champaign, IL: Office of Continuing Education and Public Service University of Illinois at Urbana-Champaign.

Kreitlow, B. W. (1990). Customers or learners? *Adult Learning, 2*(1), 7.

Kruger, R. A. (1988). *Focus groups: A practical guide for applied research.* Newbury Park, CA: Sage.

Laird, D. (1985). *Approaches to training and development.* Reading, MA: Addision-Wesley.

Lauffer, A. (1978). *Doing continuing education and staff development.* New York: McGraw-Hill.

Lenz, E. (1980). *Creating and marketing programs in continuing education.* New York: McGraw-Hill.

Lewis, C. H. & Dunlop, C. C. (1991). Successful and unsuccessful adult education programs: Perceptions, explanations, and implications. In T. J. Sork (Ed.), *Mistakes made and lessons learned: Overcoming obstacles to successful program planning* (pp. 15–28). New Directions for Adult and Continuing Education, no. 49. San Francisco: Jossey-Bass.

Malone, V. M., & Gingera, D. (1989). Managing volunteers and partnering. In D. J. Blackburn (Ed.), *Foundations and changing practices in extension* (pp. 94–101). Guelph, Ontario: University of Guelph.

Matkin, G. W. (1985). *Effective budgeting in continuing education.* San Francisco: Jossey-Bass.

Meister, G. G., & Evers, N. A. (1985, November). *Leadership and program development.* A paper presented at the American Association for Adult and Continuing Education National Conference, Milwaukee, WI.

Merriam, S. B., & Caffarella, R. S. (1991). *Learning in adulthood: A comprehensive guide.* San Francisco: Jossey-Bass.

Mezirow, J. (1963). *Dynamics of community development.* Metuchen, NJ: Scarecrow Press.

Mezirow, J. (1991). *Transformative dimensions of adult learning.* San Francisco: Jossey-Bass.

Moss, G. (1989). *The trainers handbook for managers and trainers.* North Ryde, New South Wales: CCH Australia.

Nadler, L., & Nadler, Z. (1987). *The comprehensive guide to successful conferences and meetings.* San Francisco: Jossey-Bass.

O'Donnell, J. M. (1988). Focus groups: A habit-forming evaluation technique. *Training and Development Journal, 42*(7), 71–73.

Orem, S. D., & Brue, D. F. (Eds). (1991). *Practical programming in continuing professional education: Examples for understanding and im-*

proving practice. Washington, DC: American Association for Adult and Continuing Education.

Schroeder, A. (1992). Evolving theories in legal liability: How will they affect cooperative extension? *Journal of College and University Law, 18,* 483–558.

Simpson, E. G. Jr., McGinty, D. L., & Morrison, J. L. (1987). Environmental scanning at the Georgia Center for Continuing Education: A progress report. *Continuing Higher Education Review, 51*(3), 1–20.

Simerly, R. G. (1989). A ten-step process to ensure success in marketing. In R. G. Simerly & Associates, *Handbook of marketing for continuing education* (pp. 445–451). San Francisco: Jossey-Bass.

Simerly, R. G. (1993). *Strategic financial management for conferences, workshops, and meetings.* San Francisco: Jossey-Bass.

Simerly, R. G. & Associates (1989). *Handbook of marketing for continuing education.* San Francisco: Jossey-Bass.

Smith, D. H., & Offerman, M. J. (1989). The management of adult and continuing education. In S. B. Merriam & P. M. Cunningham (Eds.), *Handbook of adult and continuing education* (pp. 246–259). San Francisco: Jossey-Bass.

Steele, S. M. (1989). The evaluation of adult and continuing education. In S. B. Merriam & P. M. Cunningham (Eds.), *Handbook of adult and continuing education* (pp. 260–272). San Francisco: Jossey-Bass.

Sork, T. J., & Caffarella, R. S. (1990). Planning programs for adults. In S. B. Merriam & P. M. Cunningham (Eds.), *Handbook of adult and continuing education* (pp. 233–245). San Francisco: Jossey-Bass.

Tallman, D. E., & Holt, M. E. (1987). Moving learning from workshops to work. *Continuing Higher Education Review, 51*(1), 15–32.

Tennant, M. (1988). *Psychology and adult learning.* New York: Routledge.

Tough, A. (1968). *Why adults learn: A study of the major reasons for beginning and continuing a learning project.* Monographs in Adult Education, No. 3. Toronto: Ontario Institute for Studies in Education.

Tough, A. (1982). *Intentional changes: A fresh approach to helping people change.* Chicago: Follett.

Trusty, F. M. (1987). Managing the tensions that go with the planning process. In R. G. Simerly (Ed.), *Strategic planning and leadership in continuing education* (pp. 103–124). San Francisco: Jossey-Bass.

Wilson, M. (1976). *The effective management of volunteer programs.* Boulder, CO: Volunteer Management Associates.

Yellen, I., & Hussey, C. (1990). Marketing for nothing. *Adult Learning, 2*(1), 8–11.

INDEX